Catch the Whisper of the Wind

Catch the Whisper of the Wind

INSPIRATIONAL STORIES AND PROVERBS
FROM NATIVE AMERICANS

Cheewa James

Health Communications, Inc.
Deerfield Beach, Florida

James, Cheewa.
    Catch the whisper of the wind: inspirational stories and proverbs from Native Americans / Cheewa James.
        p.   cm.
    ISBN 1-55874-369-3 (trade paper)
    1. Indians of North America—Social life and customs. 2. Indians of North America—Interviews. 3. Indian philosophy—North America. 4. Indian proverbs—North America. I. Title.
E98.S7J35   1995
973' .0497—dc20   97-40478
                                                              CIP

©1995 Cheewa James
ISBN 1-55874-369-3

Publisher: Health Communications, Inc.
            3201 S.W. 15th Street
            Deerfield Beach, Florida 33442-8190

Cover photograph by Grant V. Faint
Cover design by Linda Golden

This book is dedicated to my father,
Clyde "Chief" James
1900-1982 . . .
my two sons,
David J. and Todd B. Easterla . . .
and my grandson,
Tanner B. Easterla—
The four men who have most profoundly
touched my life.

CONTENTS

ACKNOWLEDGMENTS

I thank my marvelous friend and sister in spirit, Marilyn Harlan, who contacted people, set up interviews and reviewed my work—often, as she will attest, faxed to her in the middle of the night. Darlene Brown Toyobo, Concow/Yuki/Littlelake/Shoshone/Bannock, and Mary Youngblood, Aleut/Seminole, are my other sisters in spirit. These three women helped me throughout this project. The four of us will never forget our trip together through New Mexico, securing bonds of friendship between ourselves—and everyone else who had the great fortune to run into us!

I thank my blood sister Doris Hartshorn for her support. A special thanks to Jan Tilmon of KVIE-PBS, Sacramento, for her continuing encouragement and for never giving up on me. And thanks also to Peter Vegso and Christine Belleris of Health Communications, Inc., who had the vision and foresight to see the value of this book and bring it to reality. My thanks to Patty Hansen for providing the bridge to Health Communications, Inc.

Acknowledgment for help in finding interviewees for this book goes to Joy P. Effman, Karuk/Klamath; Sacheen Cruz Littlefeather, White Mountain Apache/Yaqui; Beverly Morris, Aleut; Institute for American Indian Art, Santa Fe; Linda Amelia-Chappabitty, Chinook/Cowlitz; Mark Remington; and Elaine Gloystein. Thanks to Ed Visser for his computer assistance and Stevie Kobos for editing assistance. Much of this book was put together with my two-year-old grandson Tanner on my lap. I would put a stroke in, he would take it out. Thank you, Tanner, for finally realizing that this was not the way to work together.

Two people wrote their own stories—Richard Lyman, president emeritus of Stanford University, who is also one of two non-Indians credited with a story, and my son David J. Easterla. Dave likes the company he is keeping.

This book has brought me lifetime friends. It has also brought me full circle, back to old friends lost in the shuffle of life, who will now be with me forever. I worked for Tony Reyna, former governor of Taos Pueblo, in his arts and crafts shop during my teen years. He was my most frustrating interview. Every question I would ask, he would reply, "You remember." That was a long, long time ago, Tony! Minisa Crumbo, a poet and artist who was a childhood friend in Taos, is back, and I rejoice. She writes:

Cheewa, in the tradition of the Picuris Pueblo of northern New Mexico, is the eagle's call. Chee-wa. Chee-wa.

Cheewa James was so named by her great-great aunt Jennie Clinton, who died in 1950 at well over 100 years of age, the last survivor of the Modoc War of 1872-73. In the Modoc tongue, Chee-wa means "beginning of a basket" and speaks of the orderly and methodical progression of basket construction.

Cheewa embodies the medicine of both tongues. The basket of her being is held aloft to catch the myriad voices of Native Americans as they speak with the eagle's tongue of their experiences on the earth walk.

INTRODUCTION

I walk through life now with the spirits of 56 other people in me.

In the beginning, when they opened their hearts and minds and shared their souls with me, there was an awesome feeling of responsibility. It was sometimes hard to sleep at night because of the need I felt to say everything just right so others would understand. But as I completed each story, the feeling moved from one of accountability and obligation to one of accomplishment and joy.

There were times I cried at the pain and grief I heard. Those tears were often shared by the tellers of the stories. We laughed together as we relived the pleasure and humor of times past. I felt incredible pride in sharing an American Indian heritage with these people—or using the term one of my interviewees prefers, a Pnaci heritage. I felt delight at some of the quick, dry humor an Indian can bring, reminding me of my father's own poker-face wit.

Certain general themes and philosophies run throughout the stories in this book. I must bring them to your attention. The spirit of community caring stands out as well as the giving nature of indigenous people. Also, the high regard for older people and the emphasis on family and extended family is a model we can all follow.

I am impressed at the number of American Indians who have served in the armed forces, truly serving America. I am struck by the devastation that alcohol has brought to Native Americans. It is a sadness that hits deep and must be turned around.

I collected these stories to offer inspiration, hope and belief in the human spirit. However, it must be acknowledged that there is a reservoir of history here that will prove even more valuable as time moves on. The people I have interviewed are a generation of Native Americans who have experienced some of the most difficult times in the history of their people. It has been a time of immense change and reconstruction, as indigenous people in the United States and Canada have been relocated, schooled and governed in new ways and placed on reservations.

It is here recorded for all time.

May serenity circle on
silent wings and catch the
whisper of the wind.

—CHEEWA JAMES, MODOC

Clyde L. "Chief" James
1900-1982

THE SPARK

David James Easterla, Modoc

I grew up in the small Midwestern town of Maryville, Missouri, in a house near the edge of town. I first became aware of the spark when I was about eight years old, but I was too young to realize what it was.

My grandfather, Clyde James, of Modoc heritage, was born in Oklahoma Indian Territory at the turn of the century. My mother was born on the Klamath Indian Reservation in Oregon. But I had always lived in Missouri and knew nothing of these ancestral homelands.

It was through my grandfather Clyde that I first experienced the spark. He was very Indian-looking, and because we lived far away from any American Indian communities, I was a little apprehensive of him when I first came to know him as a child. He looked different from the people around me. He had his children, including my mother, Cheewa, quite late in his life, so was an older man when he came into mine. I did not know my grandfather very well. I rarely saw him and, when I did, it was always for a short period of time. He was always traveling.

I was around him enough to know that he never seemed to get angry, had a one-liner, deadpan-face sense of humor and loved children. Grandpa Clyde was one of these drop-dead handsome men with silver hair. The widows swarmed around him.

My family would leave for several months every summer; my father was a seasonal park ranger in different national parks around the country. My grandfather came and took care of our home in the summer while we were gone. I would see him for a few days before and after our trip.

After we returned the first summer he was there, I was amazed the way this old person could be in a place for only two and a half months and know *everybody* who lived there. Everybody really liked Grandpa Clyde. I saw how people would go out of their way and take their time to talk with him. You could tell they liked and cared for him, even the people who may have met him only casually .

Over the next couple of years, I began to refer to this as the spark. No matter where I went in that town, people would come up to me and ask, "How is your grandpa?" They didn't ask how I was, or how my summer was, or how my parents were. People I didn't even know would come up to me and ask about him. How did they know him? How did they know me? And it was always so positive. People would just go on and on about him. How could he make such an impression on so many people in so little time?

It got to the point that if I saw people heading toward me with a big grin on their face, I knew they were going to ask me about Grandpa Clyde—my teachers, the man at the store, the postman, even my friends who were my age. The city gave him a baseball trophy one summer for being the best fan at the baseball games. I had never heard of such a thing. Most of the baseball players themselves don't win a baseball trophy, but some old man up in the crowd gets one. I remember thinking this was a little ridiculous. How could anybody do this or be this, especially at his age? How could he have such an impact on people?

I could go anywhere in the United States and, if Grandpa Clyde had been there, it was the same thing. A visit to my cousins in South Dakota showed everyone up there knew and loved him. The vacations out west to see my family's friends: the same thing. I remember thinking to myself that it was like he gave everybody he met a pill or something that made them feel good and positive about him, themselves, everything.

I called this the spark. After a while I could see Grandpa's spark in other people. I could tell if they had spent a lot of time with him just by watching their faces, their motions and their attitudes. The spark had the power to make people glow. It had the power to move from person to person like spreading fire in the wind. I learned to see it, but it seemed to elude me.

I've always regretted that I wasn't able to get to know Grandpa Clyde better. I know one of the most beautiful things in the world is to know and love your grandparents, as I have fortunately been able to do with my other grandparents.

Grandpa Clyde died when I was 19. I've always thought that the town knew him better than I did, and there's been an empty place in me since his death because I would never be able to get to know Grandpa.

I am a grown man now and have come to realize that I knew Grandpa Clyde better than I ever believed. Only recently I realized that the person he gave his biggest spark to was his daughter, my mother, Cheewa. Clyde James touched the life of each person who had contact with him. My mother does the same. She is him. I love her for the things she does for other people and the way she makes them feel good, the way she, too, harbors the spark and passes it on like Grandpa Clyde did. I can only hope that I may do the same.

Everything the power of the world
does is done in a circle.
The sky is round, and I have heard
that the earth is round like a ball
and so are all the stars.
The wind, in its greatest power, whirls.
Birds make their nests in circles,
for theirs is the same religion as ours.
The sun comes forth and goes down again
in a circle. The moon does the same,
and both are round.
Even the seasons form a great circle
in their changing, and always come
back where they were.
The life of a man is a circle from childhood
to childhood, and so it is in everything
where power moves.

—BLACK ELK, OGLALA SIOUX

CIRCLE OF GIVING

Ada Deer, Menominee

My mother was good and did good.

Constance Stockton Wood Deer (1904–1984) passed her agenda on to me. She was a nurse whose blood was English, Irish and Scottish. Very early she let me know that I was on this planet to help people. Although she wasn't Indian, she was very direct in letting me know that I was Indian, and had a duty and responsibility to the Menominee and other Indians.

My mother came from a long line of ministers and missionaries. My cousin went as a missionary to Colombia, South America, and then to Africa. My mother had a similar drive to serve and to explore, but her direction was not to the missions. Mother's father, my grandfather, planned for her to marry a minister's son. She rejected this and became a nurse. An avid horseback rider, she turned the tables when she went out looking for a horse to buy and liked the rider better.

That rider was an attractive Menominee man who was to become my father. Joseph Deer was born 200 years too late. He spoke the Menominee language, worked in the lumber mills, and thrived on hunting and fishing. I can see him active and successful in the old Menominee lifestyle. My dad was caught in a time warp that put him between two cultures. He was not one to talk about feelings, engage in political discussion or reach out.

My mother was the one who fed my brain, stimulated my sense of duty and willed to me her determination and fortitude. Her first contact with Indians came in the 1930s on the Rosebud Sioux Reservation, where she worked as a nurse in the BIA (Bureau of Indian Affairs) Hospital. She liked going to powwows, worked at mastering the Sioux language and loved to ride the reservation by horseback. She had a great appreciation and respect for native people and their cultures.

Looking back at it all, I think my mother had a fantasy about what reservation life would be like when she married my father. She was with a handsome Indian man who would introduce her to a dynamic, wonderful life. In reality, her transition was very rough. There was a resistance to outsiders among the Menominee, living conditions were often less than desirable, and my dad drank a lot. I remember her asking people who were drinking to stay away from us when I was as young as five years old. As for me, at an early age I formed the idea that getting drunk was a stupid way for people to behave.

I was born an adult. I suppose when you are the eldest child of five, you become the automatic care provider. That almost inborn sense of taking care of people has stuck with me over the years. It was perhaps my destiny from the very beginning.

The great motivation in my life is to serve. But I also know that serving and giving are part of a circle that includes receiving. Early in my life my tribe gave me a great gift, and it was to change my life. I went to college on a tribal scholarship of $1,000 a year. It doesn't sound like much today, but that money, coupled with the money I earned working in the college library and dining room, got me through school. My interests, influences and course work led me to social work, a profession devoted to helping people.

This sphere of receiving and giving came full circle when, still following my mother's agenda, I spearheaded the protest of the 1954 Menominee tribe's termination of tribal recognition by the federal government, resulting in the loss of our tribal status.

December 22, 1973 was a historic day for the Menominees and me. On that day, President Richard Nixon signed the Menominee Restoration Act. Most women give birth to babies after nine months. After two years, my helpers and I had given birth to a tribe federally recognized again, looking toward new tribal government and policy, and asking the federal government for protection, not domination.

In time, I became the first woman Assistant Secretary for Indian Affairs with the U.S. Department of the Interior. I find a lot of fulfillment and joy in correcting some of the world's injustices. I wonder if my mother, even in her wildest dreams, ever imagined how much I would be able to serve Indian people. I know that she is smiling down at me from the sky.

Ada Deer

WHAT IS LIFE?

Crowfoot, Blackfoot

In the spring of 1890, Crowfoot lay on his deathbed. His wife and family pressed close to his couch as his breath grew more labored. But his mind was still lucid, and he felt the surging of love around him.

Life outside his lodge was coming into leaf and bloom as he faced his final move through the arch of life to the other side of the circle. Death was coming to him as the earth itself was renewing.

Crowfoot was a Canadian Blackfoot Indian leader. He was the Indian that in his earlier years had ceded 50,000 square miles of rich Canadian land to the Canadian government. Crowfoot had done so in good faith, knowing that the Blackfoot were facing new and profound changes. He was offered what seemed to be a workable alternative for the Blackfoot.

As he lay on his deathbed, his people around him were starving. White hunters of the buffalo had moved onto

Blackfoot lands and decimated the buffalo herds. The Blackfoot were not only dependent on the buffalo for food, but the animal provided shelter, clothing, even buffalo chips for their fires. The buffalo was woven into Blackfoot theology. The death of the buffalo signaled death for the Blackfoot.

As he lay dying, his oldest daughter, standing near him in the death vigil, asked Crowfoot, "What is life?" He could have talked of death and pain and of the sorrow he and his people were feeling so strongly at this time. He could have reflected on his own feelings of guilt. He could have seen the anguish of failure.

Instead, he thought for a period of time, and a faint smile crossed his face as his old eyes lit with memories. He turned to his daughter and answered her:

It is the flash of a firefly
in the night.

It is the breath of a buffalo
in the winter time.

It is the little shadow
which runs across the grass
and loses itself in the sunset.

THE DOGS WHO SPOKE NO ENGLISH

Victor Gabriel, Washoe

My grandmother, Harriet Charlie, had dogs who hunted their own meals. They'd catch rabbits and bring them back to her house, dropping them on the porch. Grandma took the rabbits, mixed them with bread and made a stew for the dogs, who hung patiently around the porch after hunting, tongues hanging out, waiting for their stew.

I lived in San Francisco, but as a boy, in the summers I returned to the Dresslerville Colony—which is what we called our Washoe land, south of Carson City, Nevada—and lived with Grandmother. I don't know how old she was, but her daughter, my mother, was born in 1907.

I remember what little control I had over the dogs because, although they were very well-trained, they didn't speak English, and my Washoe was limited. I would yell a command out, and they'd cock their heads quizzically back and forth, as if to say, "We'd like to help, but you talk like you've got mush in your mouth."

I couldn't pronounce the Washoe names very well, either. I remember that the closest I could get to the old toothless German shepherd's name was Taxi. So that was his name. When my grandmother found him he was starving, and eventually his teeth fell out. He was afraid of storms and thunder, probably a holdover from that hard time as a puppy, when maybe someone shot at him. Washoe dogs are not allowed in the house, but Taxi was an exception. During storms, he cowered under the table and then went outside when it was over. In the whole bunch, there was only one bilingual dog, whose name was Pot-pot, another Washoe language corruption.

We used to go to Woodfords, California, for Native American Church prayer meetings. During the day, the sides of the teepees, which people had pitched for their stay, were rolled up so the breeze could cool the inside. Kids like me ran in and out, playing. The adults, who were tired from the sunset to sunrise gathering, relaxed and talked.

At one meeting in the 1950s, when I was about eight years old, an old woman dressed in calico was sitting under a pine tree with a bunch of puppies around her. "Oh, boy! More dogs!" I thought, and I went over to play with them.

"Would you like to have one?" she asked me. Would I like to have one? Would I ever! It was a little water spaniel with webbing between her toes.

It turned out that the woman was strongly suspected of being a witch. What a controversy arose with my grandmother and the other women over accepting the little puppy from a witch. The final consensus was that the damage was done. I had a new dog.

I often stayed with my Uncle Leonard and Aunt Elizabeth at the Carson Colony, along with my cousin Art, who also lived in San Francisco. Together, we'd go to the Hobo Hot Springs, where we'd swim and bathe. When it was time to start home, my aunt went on ahead to get the fire started and the vegetables and potatoes going. But my uncle, cousin and I would take the back roads, with Art and I perched on either fender with our .22 rifles. Rabbits will stop and listen if they hear a whistle, so we'd whistle, then pick off the rabbits with our .22's. We'd get back with six or eight rabbits on the bumper, skin them and give them to my aunt to complete her meal.

I can remember going to get firewood for my uncle's wood stove. It was an all-day, all-family event. The clean smell of the pines, fishing for the natural native trout, Grandma picking wild onions—memories that drift to me from the past of the simple things we did.

My grandmother had the secret. She was at peace with her baskets, a simple but fulfilling occupation for her. The Washoe are known for their fine baskets. My great-great aunt, Dat-so-la-lee (Louisa Kizer), is recognized today as the greatest basket maker of them all. I remember going down to the stream to pick willows for my grandmother's baskets. In the evenings she stripped the bark off into thread-like pieces, then rolled them around her hand like yarn. The center parts she wrapped into different lengths, and the bundles leaned against the back door.

My world as a boy was a swirl of color. At the Native

American Church meetings, I would see the tiny, tiny bead-work known as "peyote stitch," which is beaded onto the handle of a drum stick or gourd rattle. There were medicine bags with beadwork, beaded bolo ties and coral jewelry.

The colors from my boyhood I re-create today, in jew-elry. That is my profession. From the basic Navajo, Zuni and Hopi designs, I work a lot with inlay, using a combination of stones—lapis, turquoise, sugilite, variscite—to create con-temporary work that allows my imagination to soar.

I am grateful for the inspiration my heritage has given me to do these things. But that is not the greatest gift. I know today that it is the simple things that count in life. We complicate our lives seeking pleasure. We look too hard. It is there in the teepees pitched with children playing through them, dogs waiting for their stew, bathing in hot springs and feeling the love of family all around.

My heart is filled with joy when
I see you here,
as the brooks fill with water when the
snow melts in the spring;
And I feel glad as the ponies do when
the fresh grass starts
in the beginning of the year. . . .
I was born upon the prairie where
the wind blew free
and there was nothing to break
the light of the sun. . . .
Do not ask us to give up the
buffalo for the sheep.

—Ten Bears, Comanche

THE DANCER

Bill Franklin, Nishinon

I was born in 1912 in El Dorado County, California, and raised in an orphanage in Ione. I was of Nishinon (Miwok) descent, but was in the early part of my life very rootless. I would at times go back to where the Ione/Miwok people lived and stay with whomever would take me in.

At the age of 15 I entered the Sherman Indian Institute in Riverside, California, where 700 boys and 800 girls from Indian groups all over the country came for schooling. Vocational training was offered to the students there. After some thought, I decided to be either a harness maker or an undertaker! But overcrowding left only one vocational training open, so I went into the farm/ranch program. I went to school half a day and worked on the ranch the rest of the day. I learned the meaning of hard work and did things I would never otherwise have done.

One thing I'll say about Sherman: I got discipline. During 1928 and '29, I was part of the military training.

Every morning we were up at 6:00 A.M. to train. On Saturdays and Sundays we went through the regimentals and parading, showing our skill with guns. We were assigned to one of three companies: "A" company for tall boys, "B" for medium height, "C" for shorties. I was in "B" company.

We were in southern California, and even back in the 1920s the star-studded life was there. Movie companies were always looking for Indian extras, and so our parading and strutting brought out directors, producers and actors. Even the great Indian athlete Jim Thorpe made an appearance at our school. One weekend, who should appear but Mae West. Being red-blooded young men, we looked her over and began to yell, "Hey, Mae. Hey, Mae." Young men and women were selected periodically to be in movies, but no one came pounding on my door, so I guess they never had need of a 15-year-old Nishinon.

I was a cross-country runner. Some of the world's best runners, like Harry Chaca and Franklin Suhoo from the Navajo, were at Sherman. I remember an Indian by the name of Flying Cloud who ran 400-odd miles from San Francisco to Grants Pass, Oregon, averaging 65 or so miles a day. That was a feat I'll never forget. I ran every morning, but once again, no one came pounding at my door asking for this Nishinon to compete in the Olympics.

At 15, another significant event occurred in my life. To my astonishment, my father, a total stranger to me, showed up on horseback one day. He had made quite an effort to come see me, traveling some 50 miles. In those days, only horse or buggy got you places, and my father had a long ride. I found that I had six brothers and sisters. That was a good feeling, I'll tell you, to know that suddenly I had a family. I found out that two other sisters had died.

All my life I have been fascinated with the tribal dancers. When I was only 12, I danced in the roundhouse with the elders. Attending the Big Times (we didn't call them pow-wows in those days) was a great event for me. In the 1940s I started gathering up old-timers and interviewing them about the singing and dancing they did. There were only four or five left, and I knew that when they went, everything would go. I began dancing, singing and putting my regalia together. I constantly went back to the old-timers to make sure I was doing each thing right. I clearly remember one elder who said he was very resentful about what I was doing. He said that it had all been dead and unpracticed too long.

"You don't know what you're doing, Bill," he said. When I finally had everything in place and was ready to show what I knew, I asked this man to come watch. He came and watched silently.

Then he looked at me and said, "You done it, Bill." That was some of the finest praise I ever had.

There are no old-timers around any more—I guess maybe I'm one now. So I have to train the younger people in what I learned. I direct the Miwok Dance Group. I teach my troupe more than just to get out there and dance. They have to learn what songs go with what dance and what meaning there is in each dance. The dancers need to know the subtle changes in tempo and that dancers do not do what they wish. There is a pattern and an understanding.

I never did become a harness maker or an undertaker. It would appear that I was destined to fan the fire of our old customs and ways. I have taught my grandsons what I know, and they must take over because I can't get around like I used to. But although my body doesn't move as fast as it did in the old days, I was once a Sherman cross-country runner, and my heart and spirit still soar when I hear the drum beat.

Bill Franklin, late 1960s.

SHOW OF STAMINA

Jane Summers

My husband, Mike, and I first read about the Redwood Highway All-Indian Marathon, held in 1927 and '28, in an old newspaper clipping in the Kerbyville, Oregon, Museum. I was intrigued at the thought of men running for seven and a half days, averaging 65 miles each day. I was puzzled that there was so little written or known about this 482-mile race from San Francisco to Grants Pass, Oregon.

The marathons were conceived as publicity for the new Highway 101 opening up along the West Coast. The original publicity stunt, most thankfully dropped, was to bring lumberjacks in from all over the Northwest and see who could cut down the biggest redwood.

Publicity at the time touted the "natural savages" that would run. Notices of the event were put out to American Indian communities across the United States. The prize money was set at $1,000, a sizable amount in those days, and a new Buick. There were 11 entrants in the first marathon, most of them Karuks from northern California and New Mexico Zunis. One of the Zunis who ran was a 55-year-old man. The eight Karuks running had been given such names as Fighting Stag, Flying Cloud and Mad Bull.

The contrast between the two tribes was quite extreme. The Karuks had intermingled into the surrounding non-Indian community to a much larger degree than the Zunis, who were still very traditional. Before the race, the Zunis sprinkled the ground in four directions with corn meal, symbolizing good luck and success.

Small communities along the route sponsored different runners. The Grants Pass Cavemen, still in existence today, was a civic and business organization that participated in the promotion of the race. There were 15 to 20 Cavemen in the marathon itself, offering support to the eight Karuks. The Cavemen dressed for their roles, wearing animal skins and appropriate wigs, and carrying clubs. Each runner was followed by a car that carried water and supplies and that provided a place to sleep each night. One pre-race promotional photo shows the Cavemen, in costume, pictured with the Karuk, dressed in Plains Indian garb.

Training involved a turn in the sweathouse each morning, a quick swim in the icy Klamath River, and then running up and down hills. The runners were already in great shape before their training.

The marathons were run in June, which meant there was some extremely hot weather along the way. Contestants ran in leather boxing shoes, boxing shorts and tank top T-shirts, popular in that era. The race started on San Francisco's Grant Avenue and continued to the edge of the bay, where all the marathoners were ferried to the other side. From there, the marathon went straight up the coast, and seven and a half days later ended in Grants Pass. Many of the runners dropped out, but the 55-year-old Zuni was one of the finishers.

Mad Bull (Johnny Southard) won the 1927 marathon and Flying Cloud (Henry Thomas) won the 1928 event. Both were Karuk. I located Johnny Southard and talked with him. Southard was a small, wiry, lean man, obviously still in excellent shape. He was somewhere around 90 years old. He had a little home outside of Redding, California, and when I told him that I had located a film of the race, he was very excited. I arrived at his home, where he had his grandson there to watch with him. His pride was obvious, and he and his grandson were visibly impressed with the film. Southard had met a young white woman at the race who was enamored with the big winner, and he eventually married her.

When I asked what kept him going in the marathon, he seemed to see it as a personal race against Flying Cloud. "I just wanted to cut him off at the pockets." What came through to me was the great focus and determination this man still had in life. He had a "got to do this no matter what" attitude. I am not surprised he won.

There was a lot of hoopla and a lot of exploitation surrounding the race, but there was also great excitement on the part of both promoters and runners. What stands out in my mind is the remarkable training, discipline and determination of the runners. Johnny Southard exemplifies the dedication of the superb athletes who ran the Redwood Highway All-Indian Marathon.

Redwood Highway All-Indian Marathon

We are part fire, and part dream.
We are the physical
mirroring of Miaheyyun,
the Total Universe,
upon this earth,
our Mother.
We are here to experience.
We are a movement of a hand
within millions of seasons,
a wink of touching within
millions and millions
of sun fires.
And we speak
with the mirroring of the sun.

—FIRE DOG, CHEYENNE

HOW THE SENATOR GOT HIS NAME

Ben Nighthorse Campbell, Cheyenne

When I decided to run for the U.S. Senate, people said they'd never seen such fire in Ben Nighthorse Campbell's eyes. But winning wasn't what it was all about. It was important to live up to people's needs and expectations and to honor the Cheyenne name "Nighthorse" by doing the best job I could.

I'd experienced many things that helped develop my sense of competition and determination. My childhood in California wasn't easy. My mother was chronically ill with tuberculosis, and I spent much time in foster homes. Judo became an outlet for me and helped hone my competitive skills. It took me to the Olympics.

After winning the primary, the campaign machinery was ready to roll in my bid for senator of Colorado in 1992. It wasn't much to envy. We were sorely underfunded, and the significant lead I'd held coming out of the primary faded as I faced my opponent, Dick Lamm. My wife, Linda, found she had a congenital heart defect that required immediate open-heart surgery. That provided anxious moments until we knew she would be fine. The campaign lurched ahead.

The most difficult challenge was the TV debates. My opponent was well coached and a good debater. The most people said about me was that I was a natural, a diamond in the rough. Two weeks before the election, the *Denver Post* poll showed the race dead even with 44 percent each.

Looking back, I'd have to say I was depressed, tired and discouraged. Those close to me said the change was apparent. It was at this time that various warriors and religious societies of the Cheyenne began praying and holding sweats for me.

A Vietnam vet by the name of Johnny Russell, schooled in the traditional way of the Cheyenne and active in the Chief's Society, felt special steps needed to be taken. He told me to carry a tuft of an eagle father with me and to apply special red paint to certain parts of my body. He even faxed me a sketch showing me where to put the paint on my body—dots on the hand, top of the head and over my heart. When I realized I didn't have the proper paint, Johnny sent a container of the paint by Express Mail.

I talked all this over with Linda. It was a new experience for me. But we both felt there was nothing to lose and everything to win. This was my heritage and was to be embraced.

I know most people will find this hard to believe, but immediately, things began to get better. Money came in, I felt both physical and emotional strength flooding me, and my standing in the polls began to climb.

By election night, there had been a total reversal. I won by a 9.6-point margin, a landslide by Colorado standards. The northern Cheyenne felt great pride. They felt the ritual had served as a shield, given me courage and a new beginning. I couldn't argue with that.

My Indian name of Nighthorse was given to me in a 1966 Cheyenne name-giving ceremony in Lame Deer, Montana, bestowed by Alec Blackhorse, my grandmother's half-brother. It has always been important to me that my actions bring honor to that name.

It says to the world that I am a northern Cheyenne and that these are my people.

Ben Nighthorse Campbell

*Wars are fought to see who owns the land, but in
the end it possesses man.
Who dares say he owns it—is he not
buried beneath it?*

—COCHISE, CHIRICAHUA APACHE

RETURN TO THE SPIRIT WORLD

Terry Brown, Karuk
United States Marine Corps
Vietnam 1966-67

In 1991 I flew on a plane to the Marianas Islands in the Pacific—Saipan, Tinian and Rota—to do some consulting work. I had the strangest, most awkward parting from my mother, Carolyn, when she knew I was going to the Marianas. I travel often and so was puzzled by her nervousness. As the moment of my departure arrived, she pressed an envelope into my hand, asking me to read it on the Islands and do as she asked.

I am a Karuk Indian from Somes Bar, California. Because I am also a Vietnam veteran, I was contracted to assist the Commonwealth of the Northern Marianas with efforts to improve veteran services there. I would be dealing with such things as hospital, education and housing programs and service-connected benefits.

Immediately upon my arrival, as I began work on the veteran program, I hit a wall with a very headstrong Island leader who, for all intents and purposes, told me to leave the Islands on a slow boat home. That was the friendly Island way of saying thank you, but no thank you.

The days went by very quickly. I met with local leaders and community and agency heads who handled veteran matters. But every time I came close to getting something accomplished, I ran into the old hard-liner who offered no cooperation. The story was always the same. Don't call us, we'll call you.

I worked hard and did what I could in spite of my opposition. The final night before I was to leave for the mainland, I made the decision to open my mother's letter. On that last night, the local veterans had planned a banquet, and one part of it was to honor me for my work in coming this distance to help them.

I had stayed with a family that had taken me in like part of the family. The woman of the house was a true auntie, and she made me an island-flowered wreath to wear around my head that night, symbolic of their love and caring for me. That evening at the banquet, I was asked to come forward and say something to the audience.

I stepped forward, but before addressing remarks concerning my stay on the Islands, I spoke in Karuk and did my mother's bidding. Her note to me said, "Son, before you leave, burn everything in this letter. Let your uncle return home to the spirit world. He was one of the first soldiers killed as the United States came to the Marianas Islands." My uncle, I discovered, had been killed in the attack that retook the Islands and launched the final military offensive on Japan that brought World War II to a close.

Inside my mother's letter I found some of our tribe's Indian medicine *(Kishwoof)* that we burn to let the Great Spirit know humans are close by. I also found an eagle feather. As I burnt the medicine and feather that evening, my uncle's soul was released.

Most important was the reaction of the man who had created such roadblocks for me. He saw the supreme sacrifice that my uncle had made. As he approached me that evening, it was two veterans meeting and experiencing the incredible camaraderie that only soldiers on the field of combat can understand.

On subsequent trips to the Marianas, he and I worked in a new, cooperative spirit to bring benefits to the veterans of the Commonwealth of the Northern Marianas.

MU LUWETAM—
THE PEOPLE

William J. Pink, Pala

Florence Brittian, my grandmother, didn't have an easy start in life. In the early 1900s, at the age of nine, her father was shot in the back by land barons and settlers raiding their homestead. My grandmother was next to him when the bullet found its mark. Indians attempting to homestead weren't welcome.

My grandmother was a Temeku Indian, and at 14 she married James Brittian, a Cupa Indian. There were several Indian families living in the area, forming their own colony in southern California. My grandparents' home was a simple two-room house of redwood planking with a chicken coop and small barn on the property.

It was traditional for my grandparents to feed anyone who came into the house. This was true for anyone, friend or enemy. Grandmother was an excellent cook, and one of the reasons there were always people around was that there was so much good food around—fry bread, acorn mush, enchiladas, tamales and always a pot of beans.

My four brothers and two sisters and I would fight over who would help Grandmother because payment was a tortilla. We would grind tamale meat and masa (corn ground for the wrappings on the tamale) with hand-grinders. For my grandparents, things were simple, and they lived life the way it came. There were clear guidelines. I can remember that we were never supposed to sleep with the right hand over our heart because it caused nightmares.

When someone died in the colony, it was a custom to begin wailing. My grandparents did that, too, but they only wailed after someone came to the door and told them who had passed on. When my grandfather died, we wanted to follow the custom of burning the home of the person who had been lost. The fire department wouldn't allow it, so I tore my grandparents' house down, piece by piece, and hauled it truckload by truckload, 25 trips, to the ceremonial grounds. And there I burned it. I can still see my aunt, their daughter, as she threw the last piece, which had the house address numbers on it, into the fire.

My mother was a product of Indian schools and didn't experience parenting and family life. She was more like a dorm mother. She was a nurse but couldn't get a job in our town of San Jacinto because she was Indian. She had to drive 25 miles farther away, down what in those days were very poor roads. It was some years before the hospital in town, hearing that she was a good nurse, finally decided to hire her.

Two of my nephews often rode with my mother to the Soboba Reservation, near our home. She told me that on the ride there one day, the boys kept ducking down in the car. Finally, my mother asked, "Why are you ducking down?" They responded, "We're afraid the Indians might attack us." My mother laughed, looked at them and said, "Quiet. You *are* Indians."

My brother Joey died in Vietnam, and my mother could not get over it. One time at the house, I came in and she had everything set up for a birthday party. I asked her, "Whose birthday is it?" She replied that it was "just a birthday." I finally realized it was Joey's birthday. She had also lost her son Michael at birth and son Bobby to cancer.

We lived in a house that was built new in 1960. At times, we could hear kids playing at night and a baby crying. My sister-in-law and I were sitting in the living room once and I said, "The baby is crying." "No," she replied, "she's right here." But we both heard the baby cry, and even visitors occasionally heard the baby cry. Sometime soon after that, we burned Joey's and Michael's belongings, which my mother had held onto for a long time. The baby stopped crying.

Members of our family fought often and hard for our country. My uncle was on the USS *Marblehead* in World War II when it was torpedoed, and the ship drifted five months without contact. My grandparents didn't know whether he was dead or alive. All my brothers and uncles fought for America, and I did, too. It was commonly felt among other Indians I spoke to that, as Indian people, we got a raw deal at one point from the U.S. government. But this is our country and that is why we fight. I met groups of Indians from all over the United States when I went to Vietnam. There was so much stereotyping. It was assumed I would be a good scout because it is supposed to be in an Indian's blood. We were subjected to war whoops and fingers behind the head to simulate feathers.

I remember an incident that involved an Indian by the last name of Tom. I think he was a Pauite from Nevada. He was a real quiet guy from a different world, and he never drank. He talked little, never reacted much to anything. He was a constant butt of jokes and was teased unmercifully. But he still never said anything.

Then one night, the only time he ever got drunk, he put nine guys in the hospital. I guess that proved to them that he fit the stereotype of being nothing but a drunken Indian. But I'm kind of glad he did it.

It is good to be Indian and to have a strong sense of identity, but it is better to just live it and forget that someone has labeled you "Indian." We are "The People" or simply "Human Being," and in our language we are *Mu luwetam*, the first people.

When I came back from Vietnam, I spent a lot of time with our elders. They became my link to reality. Vietnam had produced tremendous trauma for me. I found when I came back that people didn't want to hear and that I wasn't accepted. I had trouble socializing and creating bonds because so many people I'd put on helicopters never came back.

I think a lot now about my grandmother, who had her father shot beside her. She had her trauma, too. Each day after I came home, I pulled more strength from my cultural beliefs. Through life I have been a soldier, a roofer, a governor's appointee, a planner, a traditional craftsman—but mostly, I think quietly to myself, I am an Indian.

TO SERVE

Tony Reyna, Taos Pueblo

I was born February 1, 1916, at Taos Pueblo, to Crucita and Hilario Reyna.

I remember my mother, Crucita, as a woman who sang and whistled at everything she did. When I think of my dad, I think of an honest man who worked his entire life, from sunrise to sunset. He was a farmer, sowing oats, corn, barley, and cultivating an array of vegetables. He had a horse and plow that he used until the 1960s, when my brothers and sisters and I bought him a tractor. As a boy I irrigated the fields, pitched hay and did all the things a young Indian farm boy would do.

The greatest gift my father gave to his eight children was the understanding that a life of giving and helping others is a good life.

He was good at setting bones, and people would come to him for help. But while his hands gave their healing gift, his tongue would do its job, too, because my father was known to all as a philosopher. Service can be given in so many ways.

Service was not so much a gift those days as a way of life. When the pueblo or someone's home needed replastering, the women would work together as a team to do it. It seems that now we hire people to do everything.

My grandmother, my father's mother, was a big part of my life, also. We respected our elders, and they contributed to our upbringing. We did not send them to rest homes. They were always with us.

When I think of those days, I think of music. People were happy and there was a lot of music, laughter and companionship accompanying just about everything we did. In the fields, when it was time to break, we'd lunch with neighbors. In the fall, when we'd bring in the corn and other crops, and because we had such a short amount of time to get the crops in before the frost, we'd work throughout the night in a communal way, with everyone helping everyone.

I attended the Santa Fe Indian School. It was very military, and we marched and drilled constantly, up and down, up and down. All that military marching came in handy when I found myself in the middle of World War II. That proved to be the ultimate service.

I served in the 200th Coast Artillery and was sent to the Philippines, where I was taken prisoner by the Japanese. I survived the Bataan Death March and was transported to Manchuria, China, where I was a POW for three-and-a-half years.

Those years were hard. They were torturous. Daily, I saw people next to me die, and the suffering was horrible. While I passed those desperate years in prison camp, thinking of my family, my home and our pueblo way of life kept me going. Because nature and its cleansing ways played an important part in my upbringing, frequently my thoughts were of the mountains and fields of the pueblo.

In Manchuria, we were put to work in an airplane factory and marched to work each day. I was a janitor. The POWs took every opportunity to sabotage the airplanes, the parts, anything on which we could have an effect. The enemy used to say, "There is always something going wrong with what you do." They didn't know how right they were. When I was released from prison camp I weighed 110 pounds, and I'm six feet tall. I spent a year in the hospital recovering.

Upon my return to Taos, I opened a shop near the pueblo where I sold Indian arts and crafts made by Indians throughout the Southwest. It's still there.

I have served twice as governor of Taos Pueblo and been active in both my community and in the art world, serving on boards and giving time and energy. My dad's belief in a life of service has had a great influence on me. Awards, whether spoken or on a plaque, don't matter. Service is a gift from the heart. Service is a lifestyle.

*You must teach your children that the ground beneath
their feet is the ashes of our grandfathers.*

*So that they will respect the land, tell your children that
the Earth is rich with the lives of our kin.*

*Teach your children what we have taught our children,
that the Earth is our mother.*

Whatever befalls the Earth befalls the sons of the Earth.

*If men spit upon the ground they spit upon themselves.
This we know. The Earth does not belong to man,
man belongs to Earth.*

*This we know. All things are connected like the blood
which unites one family.*

*All things are connected. Whatever befalls the Earth
befalls the sons of the Earth.*

*Man did not weave the web of life;
he is merely a strand in it.*

Whatever he does to the web, he does to himself.

— DUWAMISH THOUGHT,
ATTRIBUTED BY SOME TO
CHIEF SEATTLE

THE POWER OF THE SHEEP CORRAL

Andrew Thomas, Dineh (Navajo)

When the sun went down, all of our family went to bed. As in ancient times, our lives revolved around the rising and setting of the sun. We call ourselves Dineh, People of the Earth. Even our homes, adobe hogans, always have the door east to greet the sun.

All six of us children, my parents and grandmother slept in the same room, our traditional one-room hogan. It was very comforting for me as a young boy to fall asleep in the circle of my family, tucked between two sheepskins. These sheepskins, however, had to be correctly positioned on the floor. If they didn't point toward the east, I was warned, the skins would take off!

Sheep, as well as horses and cattle, are the wealth of the Navajo. My father, like the rest of our people, used them for trading since money was not in great supply.

As the eldest boy in the family, I was expected to carry on the old traditions. I learned the use of medicinal herbs to defuse bad spirits from an ailing body. I learned to pray to our Father Sky and Mother Earth.

My parents taught me many things, but one of the most important was to pray. Now, teaching young children to surrender themselves in prayer is not an easy task, especially if it means they have to get up before dawn to greet the Morning Spirits. But my father found a very effective method: he always told us, "If you don't pray early in the morning, you won't see the sun."

We thought he was incredibly powerful to be able to keep the sun from rising, but even more important, from the standpoint of children, no sun meant no playing outside, no games, no riding our horses. My father's approach worked like a charm. We jumped out of our beds immediately each morning and prayed with fervor.

We closed our days in prayer, too, giving thanks to the spirits for the things we had seen and for the tranquillity, balance and harmony of the day. This time we needed no prodding. We had one all-consuming goal: to ward off the bad spirits, the eyeless ones, who roamed in the night. We children knew that these terrifying spirits could strike you while you slept unless you had prayed and gone to sleep quickly. A child who made noises in bed and didn't go to sleep fast was a prime target. We weren't taking any chances!

Today, I find that early discipline is still with me. I now look at prayer in a new way. To me it is like insurance. You need liability, collision and fire coverage to be fully insured. Prayer is the same. For complete protection you need to pray to *all* the spirits. I suppose, as a wide-eyed young boy trying to fall asleep before the night spirits could come, I unconsciously knew I did not want to go to bed uninsured.

When each of us children was born, my parents followed the time-honored custom among Navajo people: the umbilical cord was carefully wrapped, sprinkled with corn pollen for protection and buried in the family sheep corral. Here it would never grow cold, sharing the warmth of the ewe and the lamb. It is believed that this will draw us back to the family circle in the years to come. Just as the sheep go out into the world each morning, wander over mountains and through valleys and then always come back to the sheep fold at night, so the grown child will return home to the center of his universe.

My life is in the outside world now, where I am a professional man. I help to bring together the traditional arts of our people and the rest of society. But I know I will always be a Dineh, a child of the Earth. That piece of me that once gave me life, now buried in the sheep corral, will always pull me home.

THE CREEK

Sonia Kennedy-Keller, Pétaki (Bird Woman), Seneca

The creek was right behind our house. As an adult, I can close my eyes and instantly go back there. Visualization brings the sunlight drifting through the trees onto my face. It brings the accompanying emotional rush of comfort. The trickling of the running water always sounds the same. That sound was its therapy. I knew it was solid, a piece of predictability in an otherwise shaky life. I was safe there. I was a lonely little girl with a connection to the creek and woods.

I lived the first years of my life on the Cattraraugus Reservation, near Irving, New York. The people there were mostly Seneca, *Onodowágá*, People from the Great Mountain. There was one main lodge, where the cook lived upstairs, and that's where our meals were served.

Families lived in one-room cabins with no electricity or running water. It was a community-minded group, very common among the Seneca, and during fall season the men would bring in wild turkey, and the women and children would pluck them outside on the back steps. As a child in the 1950s, I remember driving in our old woodie station wagon. If you looked through the cracks in the floorboard, you could see the ground passing underneath.

My childhood was a series of moves. We were on the Blackfoot Reservation in Alberta for a while, where I almost died of diphtheria. My parents separated someplace along the line, and finally, at the age of nine, I ended up in Auburn, California, with my father.

With five children, ages three to ten, he needed help. My grandmother, Dodie, came to live with us. She had been sent to the Thompson Indian School on the Cattaraugus Reservation in her early years. She said it was there that she learned about a world she had known very little about. She developed a strong work ethic in that world. Seneca people are very hard-working anyway, and take what they do seriously. My grandmother was the hardest-working woman I ever knew. She always made sure things were neat and clean. I still remember that she ironed Dad's underwear, the sheets and pillowcases and whatever else came along. She was an ironing fanatic.

Victoria "Dodie" Kennedy-Keller had a heart as big as the sky. No one who came through our door ever went hungry. There was always room if someone needed a place to stay.

She had been a semi-pro basketball player in her younger years. An active woman, she fell later in life and was partially crippled as a result. She had little feeling in her legs and painstakingly dragged them to get around.

Having lived most of my life around native people, I was not used to unkindness because of my skin color. I am

very dark-complexioned. One day on the school bus coming home, the children who weren't Indian began to make
fun of the other Indian children and me, doing war
whoops. Sitting near me was a little girl who was normally
a nice little girl. I think Patty just got caught up in trying
to be part of the group and wanted to fit in. In a loud voice
she yelled, "She's just a dirty squaw." It was a reflex, but
totally out of character: I slapped her across the face. In
that one hard slap, she caught all the pain that had welled
up in me from the ride home.

I arrived home sobbing and threw myself in my grandmother's arms. She wasn't happy with what I had done, but
she did understand. "Honey, don't ever be ashamed of who
you are, and don't ever try to be something you're not."
Good words that have guided my life.

When the knock came at the door, there stood Patty
with the outline of my hand still on her face. Her mother
was furious. Gram never said a word. When the woman
finally wound down, Gram straightened it out. Patty and I
became friends, and remained so. We both learned a lot on
that school bus.

Even the creek came back into my life. It was a new
creek, and my brothers, sisters and I named it Indian Falls.
Nothing would do but that Gram see it, too. "I don't know,"
she said. "With my bum legs and all."

The creek was admittedly a distance away, so we decided
to build her a wheelchair. We had one skate, a chair and a
piece of board. We nailed it all together, and Gram good-
naturedly climbed aboard. Now, Gram was not a small
woman, and even with my brother John on one side and me

on the other, the one skate in the middle made for a wobbly ride. We hit two bumps right off, both of which almost threw her. In the Iroquois/Seneca culture, women are very strong. Gram was willing to try most anything, no matter how scary. But our makeshift wheelchair tested even her fortitude, and we ended up rolling her back home.

The spirit of this woman, with her kindness and her strength, still guides me. I hold my head high and am proud to be an Iroquois/Seneca woman. I know who I am and don't try to be what I'm not.

Did you know that trees talk? Well, they do.
They talk to each other, and they'll
talk to you if you listen. . . .
I have learned a lot from trees:
sometimes about the weather,
sometimes about animals,
sometimes about the Great Spirit.

—WALKING BUFFALO,
CANADIAN STONEY INDIAN

TREE TALK

Mary Youngblood, Aleut/Seminole

I am Chaugach Aleut/Seminole and was adopted as a
baby into a non-Indian family. My parents provided a good,
supportive home for me, but it was difficult being brown in
a white world.

During my fourth- and fifth-grade school years in
Arizona, children in my class beat me, pulled my hair and
pinched my breasts—cruel schoolchildren things. When I
could outrun them, I'd hide in the bushes until it was dark,
and then I'd go home. I hated being an Indian. I wished I
could just take a bath and wash the brown skin off.

When I moved to California, I met the best friend I ever
had. She was a huge oak tree that grew in a nature area near
our home. She was my refuge and my strength, and each day
I climbed her, spending hours daydreaming. I named her
Brandi and often took pencil and paper, climbed up into her
limbs to write or draw. I loved this special tree. I told her that

I knew she'd never let me fall and would always be there to catch me.

During my painful adolescent years, I talked to Brandi, telling her my woes and hugging her. I felt comfort from her and knew not to worry about my high school prom, where no one would take out a brown girl. I had a spiritual connection to that tree.

One day I really needed to be a part of Brandi and sit in her branches. But when I got there, the tree was covered with big red ants. I had a real fear of the ants. After a lot of thought, I finally asked Brandi to ask the ants to move on. Amazingly enough, at least to everyone but me, the ants left. In the years to come when I needed to be with Brandi, the ants would leave.

Some of my friends and family thought I was nuts, but it was in this period that I realized I was different. This was the first time I felt Indian. My relationship with Brandi was something Indians could have. Being different had become a lovely thing. Even though I had been raised in a white world, the Indian had not gone away—and the Indian was beautiful! For the first time, I saw being an Indian as something positive.

It was then that things started to change for me. I began studying the classical flute, and today I play the Indian flute. My flute is hand-carved from wood. When my fingers touch the wood to play, Brandi is still in my arms.

Mary Youngblood

We are part fire, and part dream.
We are the physical
mirroring of Miaheyyun,
the Total Universe,
upon this earth,
our Mother.
We are here to experience.
We are a movement of a hand
within millions of seasons,
a wink of touching within
millions and millions
of sun fires.
And we speak
with the mirroring of the sun.

—FIRE DOG, CHEYENNE

THE WOMAN THING

Freddie Miller, Wintu/Quinault

My mother has passed from this earth. She was a
Quinault Indian woman and has found her peace. It's only
since she's gone that I finally understand her struggle for
identity. It is a struggle that many of our American Indian
women have gone through.

I didn't see her battle while she was in it because I lived for
sports and sacrificed almost everything to that. I was young,
and my eyes and ears were closed to the struggles around me.
Perhaps that's just how youth is. I was All-American for both
football and basketball in high school. In spite of my blind-
ness to her struggles, it was my mother who traveled with me
for sporting events. My dad couldn't go because of his long
hours and days spent in the woods as a log scaler.

I had my struggles, too. I felt the sting of being Indian.
In the late 1950s through 1964, there was a quota system for

minorities in baseball. Minorities could be recruited only up to a set number, leaving the teams predominately white.

I didn't understand as clearly as I do now that my mother's drinking was closely related to what many Indians went through in what I call an urban or metro crisis, when they relocated from reservations and rural areas to cities. It must be the same cultural shock I experienced in reverse when, after playing pro ball in a city, I returned to the reservation. It was such a long distance to stores, and there wasn't any television!

Many native women suffered from the transition to urban settings. Traditional tribal upbringing produces a quieter person, a woman who rarely lifts her eyes and who prefers not to speak. Indian children in general, but girls especially, when called on in open discussion, will not respond, even if they know the answer. My mother was like that. She was lost in a culture where others' perception of her was based on what she said. And she said nothing.

When I started playing basketball in the National Indian Athletic Association league after my years with the pros, there were cultural lags for many of us who had been in urban settings. For example, at the Warm Springs Reservation, we were invited into the long house, used for both cultural and social gatherings, and many of us did not know the tribal customs and the proper procedures for entering the long house.

My life has been one of relocation, transition and walking with a leg in each world. It is my mother, who struggled so with her own identity, who gave me the legacy that has guided me in these later years. She stressed to me that I don't have to answer to anyone but myself. Education has been my buffer as I mediate between my two worlds. But when I am confused, I feel her presence, reassuring me that I can be myself.

SPIRIT OF THE WHITE RIVER APACHE

Margie Grimes, White Mountain Apache

Going to my home in Cibecue, Arizona, is like going back in time. The spirit of the White River Apache dwells here.

My parents were the pillars of my life. I see myself as a female plant with my parents as my roots. My father, Francis, spoke the authentic, true Apache language, which today is very rare. I speak the more modern Apache, like almost everyone does, but I understood my father's old Apache tongue when he spoke to me.

We had no electricity when I was growing up, and we had to haul water. Some of the luckier people had donkeys, and they would fill milk cans full of water for the donkeys to take home. Once the donkey was loaded, the animal would find its way back home, where someone on the other end unloaded the milk cans. Excuse my bit of Indian humor here, but the closest we ever came to running water was when the donkeys would take off running. But when those creatures chose to stop, they were there permanently, the stubborn things!

One day a week was set aside to get wood, which the women carried on their backs. The special part of this day was getting yucca roots and shampooing our hair. We pounded the roots with a rock to soften them and then put them under water, until a lather was produced. There was nothing finer than to feel the sun on my back and the lather from the yucca as I squeezed it through my hair.

I am of the Bear Clan, which is my mother's clan. My father was of the Butterfly Clan. Among our Apache, the clan is very important because that is how you differentiate between people. The clan is especially important because it guides you in who you can or cannot marry. It is considered evil to marry within your own clan. When persons are formally enrolled with the tribe, they must list their clan, also.

We Bear Clan people have always been known as the power people, those who understand medicine. We are the ones who know the mountains, streams and canyons like the backs of our hands, and know where the medicinal herbs, plants and trees grow.

White Mountain Apache life is rich with symbolism and ceremony. In an age that is beginning to adopt thoughts like "holistic" and "healing with the mind," I know that we have always been there.

A medicine man, a counselor, becomes that only when he has overcome temptations and is tested and proved true to the way of life. It is becoming harder and harder for humans to pass that test of temptation and be truly spiritual.

Medicine men themselves are being polluted by the materialistic world. It grieves me.

Some things about our life could be models for any group of people looking for emotional and physical well-being. There is a tremendous emphasis on sharing and caring for one another.

The entrance of a girl into womanhood is a special and celebrated thing. A godmother, a role model for the girl, is selected by the family. At 4:00 A.M. on a selected morning, the family arrives to ask the godmother to honor them by guiding the daughter. An eagle feather is placed on the godmother's right foot.

The ceremony itself is conducted in an area that symbolizes the wickiup, our traditional home and the future of the girl. The community turns out to place pollen on the girl and bless her. Crown dancers paint the girl with a mixture made from ground stones, pollen and water. It is applied with a brush made from very fine and soft grass, and what is left of the paint material is sprinkled on all who have gathered so that they may also be blessed.

When the ceremony is concluded, everyone who has gathered follows the traditional Apache singers, dancing through the north, east, south and west entrances to the wickiup, moving in a clockwise direction. After the dance is finished, the men of the participating families slowly bring the four wickiup poles to the ground.

The clock truly turns back in my village of Cibecue. The emphasis on nature is still strong, and I know I live here with other living creatures that I must respect. My spirit delights in interacting with the world around me.

To me, being Indian means having all my senses awake and even possessing another sense, which most others don't have. Our ceremonies and beliefs have created structure in my life.

It is my hope that my four children and four grandchildren, being part of the modern world, are able, as I have been, to pull strength from their Apache world. May the spirit move with them.

When you get married, do not make an idol of the woman you marry; do not worship her.

If you worship a woman, she will insist upon greater and greater worship as time goes on.

—SAM BLOW SNAKE, WINNEBAGO

A NAVAJO GIRL FOR A NAVAJO BOY

Ivan Lewis, Navajo

Talk about cultural shock! Not too long ago, when I set foot on a college campus for the first time, straight off the Navajo Reservation, I walked around for four or five days before I saw another Indian. When Indian guys see another Indian, we say, "Hey, skin bro!" When I finally saw him, I latched on to my skin bro. He had an instant new friend whether he wanted one or not. He had the same kind of humor and saw things the same way I did. It gave me a lot of stability and sense of security to be around him.

I was raised in Winslow, Arizona. My father runs cattle, but he also works in a trading post in town. Because he is known by the Navajo people and speaks the language, he is important to those who don't speak English. People come from miles around to buy gas, propane, matches and other supplies. But the trading post is also a social center, a place to meet, talk and catch up on the Navajo world.

My mother raised the nine kids in our family. Until her back started bothering her, she also wove Navajo rugs. She and Dad were married in their teens. The two of them created a stable home environment for all of the family. My world is Navajo, and I am comfortable there.

But back to college. I am taking some time out trying to decide what I really want and where I am going. I'm young, unmarried and am seeking a direction. It's interesting. Just the other night at the Gathering of Nations in Albuquerque, where Indian people from all over the United States come to dance, sing and socialize, a group of my friends was questioning me about marriage. They were even throwing out names of women they thought might be good for me. I'm having enough trouble trying to make ends meet in school, and they're trying to marry me off!

Marriage among the Navajo takes some planning. First, the two families meet to make financial arrangements. The man's family offers so many horses, cows, necklaces, rugs or whatever they wish to trade. The actual ceremony takes place in the woman's home, but the groom's family will often offer to prepare the house so that it is suitable for guests, and even do minor improvements.

Extended family from both sides are invited. To begin the ceremony, the father of the bride says a prayer and the marriage couple wash their hands. The bride and groom then feed each other food from the wedding basket, which is filled with blue corn mush. The man first feeds the woman, then she feeds him. The remaining mush is shared by the groom's family, the basket going to the mother of the groom.

At the conclusion of the wedding, the elders are allowed to speak about whatever may be on their minds concerning the couple and the union. When my cousin got married, she married within her own clan, which is taboo, not an acceptable thing to do. She also had her marriage in the daytime, again not an acceptable thing to do. In our tradition, a man can never view or speak to his mother-in-law before or during the wedding. By getting married in the evening or at night, the mother-in-law can be present and watch from the background and not be seen.

Well, I mean to tell you, the elders had a lot to say about that wedding. The ceremony started at 10:00 a.m. and at 2:00 in the morning, they were still talking. I was 15 or 16 at the time, and hard as I tried to stay awake, I didn't make it to the end of the discussion.

After the wedding, the couple either moves in with the bride's parents or lives as near as possible. A newly married couple must spend the night of the wedding in the hogan with the parents. A bride and groom may not touch each other for four days.

Weddings are more than celebrating a couple's marriage. They are a chance for people to get together and socialize. Someone's car may not be running, but someone else will help them get there.

The discussion in Albuquerque the other night made me seriously think about the right wife for me. I want to marry a Navajo woman. Even though my college experience has brought me many good things, I am more comfortable with my own people. If ever I have kids, I want them to speak Navajo as I do and keep their culture alive. Finding a good job and being able to go back to the reservation would be a fine direction for me.

I hope someday soon down the line there will be a nice Navajo girl looking for a nice Navajo boy just like me!

Mother's Clan: Na'T^ho (tobacco) Dine^ee' (people) Ta'chii^nii (red running into water)

Father's Clan: To'di'ch^i'i'^nii (bitterwater)

It is not only now that woman causes trouble.
That has been since first man was.

—FATHER OF THUNDERCHILD, PLAINS CREE

WHEN COYOTE FELL
IN THE FIRE

Told to Willie Pink, who told it to Cheewa,
who tells it to you

There's a story about a group of older women who went
into the round house to gamble one evening. They divided
into two teams and went about their business.

It seems that this same evening, a young white man—
looked like what some people call a hippie—was wandering
by, heard all the noise and decided to see what all those
Indians in there were doing. It would have been more polite
if he'd knocked on the door. It sure would have been better
for him if he'd taken that route.

What he did do was climb up on the roof. He saw an
opening in the center with smoke comin' out and crawled
over to it. He peeked through the hole and saw an open fire
cracklin' away below him. Then, just like the trickster coyote might have done, he fell through the hole straight into

the fire. He must have been one surprised, scared hippie. But he was no more surprised and scared than the women down below.

He jumped left and right, tryin' to get out of the fire, but the women were convinced he was an evil spirit, and every time he'd about make it out of those hot flames lickin' at his heels, these women, screamin' and yellin' at the top of their lungs, would push him back with their canes and clapper sticks.

Now, I'm pretty sure there's a good ending to this, because there was never any tell of a man roasted to death in a round house. That hippie must have finally bounced right out of there.

Like any good coyote story, it has a moral. Mind your manners and always use the door.

Marriage among my people was like
traveling in a canoe.
The man sat in front and paddled the canoe.
The woman sat in the stern but she steered.

— ANONYMOUS

AIR WALKERS

Alice Belinda Warisose Cross Phillips, Mohawk

I grew up and live in the very small village of Kahnawake, Canada, which is populated primarily by Mohawk women and children. Most of the men leave their families for extended periods of time, up to three months, to work in modern cities far from our reserve.

Mohawk men have always been known for their lack of fear as they balance far above city streets, walking on narrow ledges and beams as if they were merely crossing a street. What it is about my people that causes them to be a cross between mountain goats and eagles, I do not know. These air-walking Mohawk ironworkers are legendary in the construction world.

My father, like his father before him, was an ironworker, a typical Mohawk "weekend dad." For a good part of his life, he had an arm that he could not straighten out because it was once smashed between two beams. Once it healed, he was back in the air, but that wounded wing left a legacy—

running water in our house. I spent my early years in a tiny house with no indoor plumbing. The injury compensation money allowed us to bring water into our home, first by drilling a well and later, as the village began to change, by tapping into the city sewer and water line.

My mother was like my sister. She was 16 when her first child was born. By 21 she had five children, and eventually nine children. I always say that's what happens when men go away and only come back once in a while.

My mother, Christina, was Irish, Scottish and Welsh. Although my father was Mohawk, he was gone so much that I never learned the Mohawk language in my home. I was related to half the town. Because this was a sea of women, communal living was our lifestyle. Out of respect for older people, we called all the women "auntie." With men so absent in our lives, women were strong role models. Every New Year's, all the women would bake—meat pie, pork hash with potatoes under a crust, mashed turnips, fruit cakes and smaller finger foods for the kids. The whole community would eat together, and it went on from 9:00 in the morning until 9:00 at night.

I married a Mohawk man, but he did not go the way of the ironworkers. We made the decision that he would find work that would allow him to be home. We have a daughter and two sons. The two boys were enrolled in Mohawk Immersion School, where they were, true to the school's name, immersed in Mohawk thinking and language. Both learned Mohawk, and as they did, so did I because it had been lost in our family. At first they laughed at my efforts because I would get tongue-tied on the longer words, but then it became clear that the more I learned, the more I could help them with their homework. They didn't laugh so much then. The way of life is to never stop experiencing new things, and that's how I feel about learning my native language, even though I am pretty old to learn. When my two-year-old daughter is ready to learn, I'll be able to help her much more.

The traditional way of the Mohawk is to belong to a clan, such as bear, wolf or turtle. The clan is determined by the lineage of the mother. Because my mother was not Mohawk, I had no clan and could not pass that on to my children. But at the immersion school, both of the boys were adopted into clans. They are in different clans. Being typical boys, 18 months apart in age, if one was in one clan, the other wanted to be in a different one!

I am a strong believer in natural medicine and healing with herbs and plants that the medicine men use. The medicine people know what to pick, whether to grind or boil it and how to use it. This knowledge is not generally known, but passed on only to those chosen by the medicine people.

The trend today is for everyone to go back to natural cures. Native people have always had and used nature. We don't abuse nature. Our land is very important. It is our life —the roots of our way. Without land, we don't feel right. It's all slipping away so quickly, though. My husband used to hunt, and I picked wild raspberries right next to our home. In 12 short years, it's all filled up now. Where the government once gave each Indian a half-acre of land for the yard, it now gives out a lot only 80 feet by 120 feet. There is a regulation about living on the reserve if you marry outside the

Mohawk. My brother married a non-Indian and had to move away. It used to be that only Mohawk women who married non-Indian men had to move. But since 1980, it has applied to men, too. That only seems right to me.

As land slips away and time seems to be going so fast, I hold on to what I cherish for my children. We have to look ahead seven generations to make sure our children have land. Above all, we have to teach them to respect that land.

LET THE SPIRIT OF THE EAGLE COME IN

Minisa Crumbo, Potawatami/Creek

I was raised as a citizen of the world and a child of the universe. Although both of my parents are of American Indian descent, they also both have European blood, and I have at one time or another drawn heavily on my French, Irish and German heritage. I identify with blood lines as well as human experience.

My father was the internationally known Potawatami artist, Woody Crumbo, noted in the Indian art world for his detailed paintings that document the costume and ceremony of the Plains Indian. The memory I have of my father from many years ago, when we lived in Taos, New Mexico, is of a stocky, black-haired man, paintbrush in one hand and ladle in the other.

Maybe the world saw the artist, but to me he was a master of highly individual soups and stews. My mother was an elementary-school teacher, and while she was at work he would paint at home and put his pot of food on to cook through the day. My brother, Woody Max, my mother, Lillian, and I would come home to Crumbo Stew. When I think about it, he was before his time in how he saw traditional gender roles.

As a girl, I was trained rigorously in the traditional war and eagle dances, which were more men's dances. My dad drummed and I danced my little heart out. He talked about the homage I paid to Mother Earth with my tapping footsteps. That was the beginning of my training in and learning respect for the environment.

I brought all my life and energy to bear on what I was doing at that time, practicing long hours and often dancing to exhaustion. I learned the importance of duty and commitment. The dance taught me to move beyond the physical and mental and to integrate the spirit—in my father's words, to allow the spirit of the eagle to come in. That has to applied to everything I have done in life. Once during the dance training, I asked him if girls did this. "They can if they want to," was his answer, and it became even more important to me that I work with him.

"Honor yourself in the present," he always said, "but bring forward that which is worthy from the past." As a boy, he had been adopted by the Kiowa and was very knowledgeable about that culture, too. A flute player and maker, he carried the Kiowa flute medicine for 40 years. What that means is that a person, once found worthy, is designated to carry forward a particular tradition. It is insurance against loss of that knowledge and a good way to preserve culture.

My father was an early and foundational part of my life. As a child I would watch him paint, even going with him as he did large murals, like the ones at the Philbrook Art Center and Gilcrease in Tulsa. In my 30s, I began my own art career. I let the spirit of the eagle come in.

Taos, my childhood home, is a well-known art center. I remember in the 1950s my parents throwing my brother and me in the car for regular outings to visit other artists in town—Bert Phillips, one of the pioneer artists in Taos, always dressed in a suit and referring to me in his Brooklyn accent as "the little goil;" Illa McAfee, best known for her spirit horses dancing in the clouds, who always made sure that her husband, a shell-shock victim of World War II and wheelchair-bound, was a part of the group; and so many more. I wonder if all parents know, as mine did, how much it means to include a child in the world around them.

As a family, with jeep, tent, my dad's rod and reel and a three-legged Dutch oven that sat high over the fire for cooking, we would take off. We let the spirit of the eagle come in as we experienced a love of the land.

My mother opened my mind to the world. She was my first-grade teacher at the Taos Pueblo Day School. Her gift was knowing that people need to see clearly and be seen truly. That power made her a superior teacher. From Dick and Jane to the literary masters of the world, she brought books to me.

She stimulated my mind so that I wanted to know, as I grew older, why the world worked the way it did and how to bring spirit to my life and the lives of others—how do we let the eagle in? My quest for answers has led me to an exploration of women's ways. The early literary grounding from my mother was invaluable to me as I worked on writing *Beloved Woman*, a contemporary guide to traditional women's ways.

Early medicine teachers were men. In those years of my life I thought that men demonstrated greater power than women. I wondered why men seemed to have more fun, more movement and more interesting lives. Even with the positive image of women that my father gave me, I wondered.

I am now on a medicine path that deals with the mystery and beauty of the woman's way. As an artist and poet, I have combined art with my mother's feel for literature and use both to express what I find on my path. I help women search for and secure harmony and balance through honoring women's bodily functions in an orderly and consistent manner. This pathway leads women toward unification of mind, heart, body and spirit.

I have traveled so many paths in my life. I have seen and felt so many things. I am grateful for the guiding hands of my parents. They have shown me the way to let the eagle in.

Minisa Crumbo

READER/CUSTOMER CARE SURVEY

If you are enjoying this book, please help us serve you better and meet your changing needs by taking a few minutes to complete this survey. Please fold it & drop it in the mail. **As a thank you, we will send you a gift.**

Name: _____

Address: _____

_____

Tel. # _____

Gender: ____ Female ____ Male

Age: ____ 18-25 ____ 46-55
____ 26-35 ____ 56-65
____ 36-45 ____ 65+

Marital Status: ____ Married ____ Single
____ Divorced ____ Partner

Is this book: ____ Purchased for self?
____ Purchased for others?
____ Received as gift?

How did you find out about this book?

____ Catalog
____ Store Display
Newspaper
____ Best Seller List
____ Article/Book Review
____ Advertisement
Magazine
____ Feature Article
____ Book Review
____ Advertisement
____ Word of Mouth
____ T.V./Talk Show (Specify) _____
____ Radio/Talk Show (Specify) _____
____ Professional Referral _____
____ Other (Specify) _____

What subject areas do you enjoy reading most? (Rank in order of enjoyment)

____ Women's Issues   ____ New Age
____ Business Self Help ____ Aging
____ Relationships   ____ Altern. Healing
____ Inspiration   ____ Parenting
____ Soul/Spirituality ____ Diet/Nutrition
____ Recovery   ____ Exercise/Health
____ Other (Specify) _____

What do you look for when choosing a personal growth book? (Rank in order of importance)

____ Subject   ____ Author
____ Title   ____ Price
____ Cover Design ____ In Store Location
____ Other (Specify) _____

When do you buy books? (Rank in order of importance)

____ Xmas   ____ Father's Day
____ Valentines Day ____ Summer Reading
____ Birthday   ____ Thanksgiving
____ Mother's Day
____ Other (Specify) _____

Where do you buy your books? (Rank in order of frequency of purchases)

____ Bookstore   ____ Book Club
____ Price Club   ____ Mail Order
____ Department Store ____ T.V. Shopping
____ Supermarket   ____ Airport
____ Health Food Store ____ Drug Store
____ Gift Store   ____ Other (Specify)

Additional comments you would like to make to help us serve you better.

_____
_____
_____

Thank You !!

A SILVER BELT

Cheewa James, Modoc

I wandered into a small Indian shop in the foothills of the Sierras in Northern California and struck up a conversation with the Native American woman who owned the shop. My own American Indian heritage and love of Indian jewelry led me to tell her of the pain I had suffered when my mother's silver Navajo concho belt was stolen.

My mother, Louella Mueller James, did not speak English until her teens. Her parents were immigrants from Germany. Although not of Indian blood, she was the one who preserved the history and all the lovely Indian arts and crafts that were handed down in our family. My mother had worn her concho belt almost every day of her life. It was handed down to me when she had passed through the arch of life to the other side.

My mother was a dramatic, articulate, creative woman. I remember as a small girl putting my arms around my mother's waist and feeling the warmth of her body through the silver platelets. Having her belt gave me great comfort after her death.

As I talked with the Indian woman, I could sense her empathy. But when I finished expressing my grief, her message was not the one of sympathy I expected. What she gave me was a new beginning and an insight into my mother.

"Remember," she said, "the true gifts you were given, things of the spirit. Don't ever cry over things that can't cry over you."

My mother is not a belt. My mother is reflected in the woman who now stands in her place—me. My true heritage is in the talents and strengths that she left to me.

I no longer cry over a thing that can't cry over me. I cherish the fortitude and love a woman left to me.

Louella Mueller James

Love songs are dangerous.
If a man gets to singing them, we
send for a medicine man
to treat him and make him stop.

—ANONYMOUS, PAPAGO

FIRST LOVE

Sherrie Bowman, Laguna Pueblo

Boy meets girl in many different ways among Indian people. Powwows, Big Times and Sings all provide great opportunities. But my mom took the long way around.

It all started in the Albuquerque Indian School during the eighth grade, when she met the love of her life, Albert, a handsome young boy from the Sandia Pueblo. They dated throughout their high school years. After graduation, Albert joined the Navy. Mom signed up, too, hoping she could be near him, but instead, they lost touch.

Two years later, Albert suddenly appeared at my grandparents' door with an engagement ring. My mother's surprised parents had a surprise of their own: my mother had married someone else. Albert was shocked but undeterred. He sent her birthday cards for a long time afterward.

Years later, after her divorce, Mom returned to my grandparents' home at the Laguna Pueblo with us children. One day, when I was 15 years old, I looked out our front window and saw a red and white pickup truck that was towing a U-Haul trailer pull up in front of our house. My mother looked at the man walking up our path and gasped, "I don't believe it!" She dashed madly to the bedroom to fix her hair. It was Albert. They found that the spark was still there, and even the addition of five children didn't snuff it out. Soon they were married, and he became a wonderful dad to us.

THE THREE ROBERTS

Robert Smith, Tututini

I was three years old when I met my grandmother, in 1913. Her Tututini Indian name was Prairie Flower, but she was known as Jane. When I was a small boy, she hauled me around in a little cart that she had earmarked for my cousin Sammy one Christmas. But he was run over by a train before the holiday came, and so I filled the cart.

She had a friend by the name of Mrs. Gus Root, who had three tattoos stroked down on her chin, a Tututini custom. Funny, the things that stick in your mind when you are a child.

My dad, my grandfather and I were all named Robert Smith. My dad dropped out of school in the fourth grade. His life as a youth took him all over the United States; he hopped rides on trains, cooking along the tracks. He was in Alaska during the gold rush and spent some of his life as a boxer, boxing under the name of Jimmy Sullivan. I guess he was fairly successful at that. I remember he said his last fight was fought to a draw. He was an adventurer, hungry for excitement.

His father, my grandfather, was very much the same, as far as I can figure. Robert C. H. Schmidt was born in Germany in the early 1800s and became a watchmaker. But like so many young men of his time, he left his native land to escape military service.

Adventure and fate brought him aboard a ship to the mouth of the Chetco River, off the shore of northern California. There, in 1854, the ship was harbored, and Robert, along with two other men, ventured ashore to explore the area. It is here that my grandparents met. It seems that Robert was a bit too adventuresome, and ended up being taken captive by the Tututini Indians in that area.

He was spirited away and hidden by Prairie Flower, the same older woman who pushed me around in Sammy's cart. His ship lay off the shore, the captain fearing that my grandfather had met with trouble, but afraid to send a search party ashore. Prairie Flower managed to get Robert's cap, with a message written on it, to the captain, letting him know that my grandfather would slip out of hiding when he could and join the ship on up the coast.

My grandfather finally rejoined the ship and was supposed to have gone back to Germany. I've always been very grateful that he couldn't get his savior, Prairie Flower, out of his mind, and made the decision to go back to her. He did that and married her, Indian fashion. Later, when she was threatened with being sent to the Siletz Reservation, he went with her down to Crescent City, where he married her again in the legal courts. They raised 11 children. The couple remained together throughout their lives.

Two distinct branches of the human tree crossed on a beach off the coast of California. It is a true story of this great country we call America.

Training began with children
who were taught to sit still and enjoy it.

They were taught to use their organs of smell,
to look when there was apparently nothing to see,
and to listen intently when all seemingly was quiet.

A child that cannot sit still is a
half-developed child.

—LUTHER STANDING BEAR, LAKOTA

SPIRIT OF THE DEER

Stan Padilla, Yaqui

My life as a male descendant of the Yaqui Indians brought with it the traditional first hunt, the coming of manhood. The Yaqui are deer hunters and deer dancers.

I remember clearly the day I killed my first deer. It was also the last deer I ever killed.

My family lived in California, far from the homeland, so I grew up with many different tribes. That intertribal background accounts for many of my feelings today about the relationship that all people have to one another, regardless of their tribe, their race or their country. That early experience also extends to my feelings of the inter-relatedness of all living things.

All my extended family—parents, grandparents, aunts, uncles—lived and worked together. We raised our own food and livestock, and we were hunters in the Yaqui tradition: bear, pheasant, dove and, of course, the deer.

During peach season the family worked cooperatively,

picking the fruit and boiling the peaches in huge outdoor pots. My life was family. It was a happy life. Harvest time especially brought everyone together, and it was then that the older people received special attention. We paid them great honor. Their special lifetime relationship with the earth offered guidance to all of us and helped us to better work the land.

But I must talk about the deer. It was the deer that was to form my true manhood, that first hunt that was to bring me to my chosen calling as an artist. This was not at all what was expected of a Yaqui deer hunter.

Among the Yaqui, the killing of a first deer was the coming of age—something like a bar mitzvah or being drafted into the military. Support came from the hunters' circle, which was made up of family members. This circle prepared me for my first hunt. It offered strength, and a release from guilt, by presenting the concept that the using, taking and eating of other life was in reality a sharing.

The day of my hunt was cold, and the darkness before dawn was total. The beginning of the hunt meant sitting very still. Patience, patience, patience . . . and then fear and trepidation began to set in. My imagination turned logs into bears. Each noise filled my heart with dread. The gradual lighting of the forest brought tremendous relief to me.

Then I had to begin listening, intensely and totally. I listened the way I was trained. Listening gives a hunter the quality of how big the animal is, the direction it's coming from, where it's going. When I finally heard the deer come up the trail, I felt fear again and my heart started pounding. It pounded louder than my thoughts.

Then the deer was there in front of me. I shot the deer and the deer crumpled to the ground. I felt triumph, completion, success . . . and then suddenly, a great sadness. What a mingling of emotions I had: life and death, creation and destruction. An animal had lost his life for me so I could have a little more in my life. I was overcome with a spiritual question: what is life?

Then came the grueling responsibility of cleaning and gutting. The intricate knowledge of my father and grandfather came into play—what to cut, how to cut—skills and techniques of the hunter. To me, a bewildered boy, it was easier to kill than to do the rest, to put my hands inside of the deer and clean the body.

I felt pride as a man, a hunter, a contributor to the family, a giver of meat. Within my society I had come of age. I was where I was supposed to be. Yet I was haunted by the way that deer and I had looked at each other. In the days to follow, his image would suddenly flash through my mind while I was working. I could feel his breathing. His spirit was with me. I did not know what it meant or what to do with this burden I carried.

It was then that my grandfather was taken from me. With his going, the deer came back into my life. Grandfather had kept the antlers and skins from all the hunts in his barn. With his death, the remains of the deer went back to the hunter who made the kill.

In getting the deer, I gained a part of myself back. The deer had taken a part of me with him when he died. I got it back when I went to the barn for the hide and antlers. My cousin tanned the hide, and I used my growing gifts of the

artist to paint it. The spirit of the deer had helped me tran-
scend the warrior way of thinking.

Coming to manhood taught me the fragility of life in
that moment of living and dying in the forest. I know now
that I don't have to kill again. Coming to manhood taught
me respect for life and the need to be in balance. I learned a
man must be powerful enough to lead a child, but also strong
enough to kneel down beside that child and play.

It may be hard for others to understand, but for me it all
came very clear. The spirit of the deer entered my art work
and remains there to this day. The spirit has allowed me to
express unseen feelings and put ancient forms in a new, contemporary expression.

Those fingers that once grabbed a gun and pulled a trig-
ger are now guided by the spirit of the deer to draw, paint
and sculpt.

JOURNEY TO THE CLAY

Robert Naranjo, Santa Clara

My father always said, "None of this Indian time for me." What he meant was that he planned to be on time and expected me to do the same.

My father, Juan, worked with the Bureau of Indian Affairs for 37 years, and if he was supposed to be there at 8:00 A.M., you looked for him around 7:00 or 7:30. After he retired, he worked at the tribal office at Santa Clara as a custodian and was always bothered by people who would pick up their paychecks in the morning and be gone by afternoon. My dad role-modeled the ultimate in responsibility, and it has guided me through life.

We lived in a wooden frame house with a basement and a big coal stove in Dulce, New Mexico, where he worked. When I look at that house today, I marvel at how such a small house seemed so big to me as a boy.

Much of my childhood was involved with sports because my dad was an athlete and an outdoorsman. I don't remember a time that my dad wasn't playing baseball. He played in the Indian league as a catcher. At one point, my older brother was pitching and my dad catching. That was quite a family event for all of us. Dad was a heck of a catcher. Because that position is really hard on knees, I especially admired him when he played on the Dulce team as an older man. He just wouldn't give up.

He was an extraordinary hunter, where patience and persistence are so important. If it would take most hunters 20 minutes to walk someplace, it would take him an hour because he moved so cautiously and quietly, always listening intently. I used to follow after him, carrying water in a canteen and rope to string the deer.

One morning we went out hunting, caught our deer and were on our way back when we came upon another deer lying in the grass. Very carefully, we moved up on the deer. "Is he dead?" I whispered to my dad.

"I think he's breathing," Dad murmured in my ear.

I touched the deer's hoof with a tentative finger. What a thrill to touch a live deer. Feeling encouraged, I reached out to feel his wet and velvety nose.

The deer must have smelled us, because at that moment, the deer reared straight up in the air, taking me with him. I will never know whether the deer, my dad or I was scared the most, but for many years, my dad and I shared many a fond chuckle over that deer.

Dad was one fantastic fly-fisherman too. I remember the time he taught Mr. Powdrill, one of the administrators at our school, the fine art of casting. I was on the bank watching as Mr. Powdrill, standing in the middle of the stream, tried his best to bring in the big one. My dad was standing on the bank when all of a sudden, smooth as could be, he whipped a line right into the water between Mr. Powdrill's legs. Within seconds, he had a catch. I still laugh to myself, after all these years, when I think of Mr. Powdrill's face.

My life wasn't as smooth as my dad's casting. Not knowing what to do with life, I decided to join the Army when my brother re-enlisted. That was in 1961, and in 1965 I re-enlisted. People used to ask me why I did that. I told them it felt so good to be out the first time, I wanted to see how it felt the second time.

When I did come out, I entered the truck-driving world and drove in the oil fields in the Four Corners area of New Mexico. I switched to logging trucks, and even though this may sound like a small thing, I got tired of changing tire chains in the mud and finally quit.

It was at this point that a different kind of mud came into my life. It was clay. My mother encouraged me to learn the ancient Santa Clara craft of pottery-making, and my Aunt Julia became my mentor.

These were good days in my life. I started with little bears, turtles and figurines and from there learned how to make the beautiful Santa Clara pottery known as "black on black"—carvings or highly polished black designs on black pottery.

I soon was selling at the Santa Fe Indian Market. Aunt Julia sold there, too. I shared my space with her, which not only brought me a great selling partner, but offered me an opportunity to repay Aunt Julia for her guidance.

I've arrived in some ways. There's been good publicity about my work. I have regular customers who buy my pottery.

But life is constantly about being humbled. One day I was leaving the Governor's portal, where I sometimes sell, and was packing my pottery in the front seat of my car. I had placed a load on the passenger seat side of the car, locked the door and slammed it. As I turned to go, I was brought up short by the fact that I had slammed the car door on my waist-long braids. This Santa Clara potter had to squat by the door until a passer-by graciously offered to unlock the door from the other side and release my braids.

It is satisfying to be creative and produce the best I am capable of producing. I work for myself, and although I do give people an idea of when they can receive their pottery piece, I always let them know that the spirit is what moves me, and I follow that. Sometimes I'll shape the clay the way I want, but it speaks to me. "Hey, Robert, I want to be something else."

Robert Naranjo

THE LITTLE PEOPLE

Wilma Mankiller, Cherokee

The Cherokee relative who impressed me most was my father's Aunt Maggie Gourd, who lived about a mile and a half from our house. She had a striking, intelligent face and wore her dark hair pulled back. She spoke English fairly well. She was a marvelous storyteller, and many of my lessons in life came from her.

It was from Maggie that my brother Johnny and I were first to hear about the Little People, *Yunwi Tsunsdi*, who live in the woods wherever Cherokees live. The Little People look like Cherokees but are small, only about three feet tall. If anything is found in the forest, Cherokees assume that it belongs to the Little People. *Yunwi Tsunsdi* are often described as "secondhanders" by the Cherokee because what is found in the woods was once owned by the Little People, and what the Little People see in the woods belongs to them.

Johnny and I were frequently asked to watch over our younger brothers and sisters while the older ones worked.

But we became a little careless about our responsibilities, and Aunt Maggie tried to impress on our young minds the importance of taking that task seriously.

That's why one afternoon she told us the tale of the young Cherokee man and woman who took their baby into the woods. They spread their blanket on the ground and placed the baby on it. While the baby dozed, the couple moved some distance away and built a campfire so they would not disturb the child's dreams. They built a fire, and when it was going well, they returned to the blanket for the baby. The infant was gone and, search as they might, it appeared the Little People had claimed the baby.

Johnny and I listened, with rounded eyes, as I recall. What I do remember very clearly is that we watched our brothers and sisters with a new sense of dedication.

Wilma Mankiller

*If you do bad things, your children will
follow you and do the same.
If you want to raise good children,
be decent yourself.*

—In-the-Middle, Mescalero Apache

*Good acts done for the love of children become
stories good for the ears of people from other bands.
They become as coveted things, and
are placed side by side
with the stories of war achievements.*

—Social tradition, Assiniboine

*Do not speak of evil, for it creates curiosity
in the minds of the young.*

—Lakota proverb

*Lose your temper with a child and
you will age in sorrow.*

—Algonquin proverb

REFUGE IN A STORM

Terry Gomez, Comanche

When life piles in on us, we seek our refuge in different ways.

When I talk about life piling in on me, I am referring to the terrible times I suffered at the hands of my father, who was an alcoholic. I spent a lot of time and energy finding ways to avoid him. My refuge was in two places: my grandparents and my reading and writing.

I lived in a small rural town in Oklahoma. The Comanche people there had allotments rather than reservations. I had a large extended family. Not much happened that didn't involve everyone. I can still see the old people who would gather in groups outside in good weather and talk.

Hand games were a part of life. One involved holding two bones, a winning and a losing bone, one in each hand. The opponent would have to guess which bone was which. We kept score on boards with holes in which we put sticks when someone guessed correctly.

My grandparents' home was truly a refuge. I was there because my mother worked and was gone a lot. Above everything else, I appreciated the non-judgmental, accepting way of my grandmother. It contrasted sharply with the strictness and cruelty I suffered from my father. Grandmother tried to compensate. She allowed me great freedom, and I would roam the land near the house with a sense of joy and relief.

My grandparents had a three-room house with no running water. We drew our water from the well. Grandmother sewed, quilted and did beadwork. She was a great cook, and I well remember her boiled meats, especially tongue, and Indian fry bread.

Oftentimes, after I had fallen asleep, my grandfather would slip into my room, bundle me up in blankets, and he, my grandmother and I would drive into Apache Oklahoma, where they would play poker into the wee hours. I'd lie on the couch, watching the fire shoot its shadows against the wall, while the older people huddled over the table with their cards. I always felt so warm, happy and loved when we went to play poker. When it was time to go, they'd wake me, gather me up and we'd head home.

I found refuge, too, in the escape world of reading and writing. Books opened doors for me. Sometime in my early teens, I won a writing contest on the subject "Why We Should Preserve the Forest." It was the spark I needed to start putting my own words down on paper. Contests like that can change a young person's life.

I left home at 19. My life took me in many directions, from job to job, but the turns in the road finally straightened out. There was nothing to escape from now. I made a serious commitment to writing. I was going to write not to escape, but because I really wanted to write about issues relevant to native people in contemporary society.

When life dealt its storms to me, I found refuge in the heart, with my grandparents, and refuge in my mind. Those are good places to go.

RETURN OF THE *PNACI*

Val Shadowhawk, Cree, Blackfoot,
Missouria, Choctow

My feet are where it started and where it has come full circle. When I had just learned to walk, a baby-sitter left me in the tub alone. I turned on the hot water and was severely scalded. It was a close brush with the blue world, the land of death. Our landlady saved my life, but my feet suffered severe damage.

I spent a year in the hospital with second- and third-degree burns and tissue damage, and my parents were told I would never walk again. My mother was only 16 when I was born and already had two babies younger than me. A crippled child was a frightening burden for a girl that young. My father was in the Coast Guard and moved around a lot, so when I was released from the hospital, I went to live with my dad's mother. My Grandmother Virgie was of the Missouria tribe, the southernmost part of the Sioux nation.

Early childhood memories are almost always dim, but I

do remember most clearly Virgie rubbing my poor withered feet. It was physical therapy, yes, but it was much, much more. It was bonding and the touch of affection that carried me through the 16 years I lived with her. Quite frankly, no one could pry me away from her, and due to the circumstances of my physical disability, I was allowed to stay with her.

Through massage therapy and constant rubdowns, my feet began to heal. My step-grandfather, Glenn Williams, a Creek, helped me learn to walk again. He would stand ten feet from me and hold his arms out. "Come here, Little Val, walk to me, son." I would do it, and he'd swoop me up into his arms.

In my early teens, I started going to powwows. Those feet and legs that now could walk were filled with the desire to be out there with the drums. Let me tell you, when the drums started, I had a physical reaction. My scalp crawled as though little ants were moving there, and my spine felt as if it was on fire.

I was destined to be a dancer. I dance today for all those who did not get a chance to dance. There was a period of 50 years or so, starting in the 1880s, when the native languages were discouraged. Indigenous people in the United States were relocated, schooled in new ways and placed on reservations. The drums were more quiet then.

We have been going through a time of reconstruction. We are coming back, but we do not come back as Indians, a term applied by others. We come back as the *Pnaci*—the descendants of the old ones. I use that term now. I feel good about the way it sounds.

I am a straight dancer, which is a dance of the Southern Plains traditionally danced by the Comanche, Missouria, Kiowa, Ponca, Osage and Omaha, among others. It is a specialty dance, a storytelling art form performed by warriors to honor warriors. Today, if you are not a veteran, you dance to honor relatives and friends who are veterans. I carry a stick to touch the ground, anchoring me and honoring the earth. The traditional otter drop or trailer that I wear on my regalia is worn from the neck to the ground and denotes a warrior.

When I danced my first dance, my father gave me a lock of hair from my great-grandmother that had originally been sent to my grandmother on her 31st birthday. My grandmother gave it to my dad. I have placed it on my dance stick. My great-grandmother's spirit goes into the circle when I dance. She is with me.

The passing of tradition, the connection of ancestors and the honoring of what has gone before gives wholeness to an individual and continuity to a culture.

There is a healing in the drum and a call that reaches to the center of my heart. It draws me. The drum has been with the Pnaci forever and reaches back in time. It is the gateway to the other world where ancestors dwell and spirits rest.

I dance to be in the circle with relatives and friends. I dance to honor others. I dance in remembrance of the remarkable past of the Pnaci.

Most of all, I dance to express thanks that I have feet that let me dance.

*We who are clay-blended by the Master Potter
come from the kiln of Creation in many hues.*

*How can people say one skin is colored,
when each has its own coloration?*

*What should it matter that one bowl is dark
and the other pale, if each is of good
design and serves its purpose well.*

—POLINGAYSI QOYAWAYMA, HOPI

THE CHEROKEE GIRL ON THE HORSE

Daphne Moody, Cherokee

It is said that my father fell in love with my mother the day he saw her ride bareback in the wind, her long, black hair whipping behind her, her lithe body twisting with the movements of the horse, and her eyes full of merriment and abandon. And it's true: that's the day my properly raised English father fell in love with my Cherokee mother.

What a joy she was to us all. What gladness she brought to my early years. As I grew up she taught me how to pick a mess of greens, as she called them. That would mean going out and gathering clover and lamb's tail, narrow dock and many other things that unfortunately have passed from my memory.

I do remember the tea that came from sassafras roots. We would dig the roots, dry them and then brew the most delicious tea. We would sweeten the tea with sugar and thick, rich cream. My mother and I would link arms and drink our tea and talk.

Mother taught me to respect people in all walks of life. She would tell me that each human being had a heart and soul. She said that we all hurt the same, and we all need recognition.

My father bought our land from his parents, and only a fence divided our land from my grandparents. Grandma did not approve of Mom being an Indian and would not accept her into her life. When the nine of us children came along, we were sorted very rapidly by Grandma into the wanted and the not wanted.

One of my sisters had long, blonde curls, and Grandma's love for her was complete. I was one of the dark, brown-eyed ones, so she never hugged or even spoke to me— except when she told me to stand up straight. Grandma's ancestry was a straight line to the lords of England, and she did indeed think she was Queen.

Grandpa, on the other hand, was loving, and cared about us all. But he was afraid to show affection when she was in the room. She would never give us fruit from the trees, but Grandpa would set apples on a big gatepost near the road so we could eat them on our way to school. We weren't even allowed to drink from the spring.

As a young child, I never knew why she did not like me. It wasn't until later that I knew it was because I looked Indian, like my mother. When I was ten, my grandmother moved away. I never saw her again until the day of her death.

She had an effect on my mother. As a small child, I saw my mother begin to move more and more away from acknowledging her Indian blood. The young Indian girl with twinkling eyes that rode in the wind and stole my father's heart moved further and further into obscurity. Mom tried to forget she was an Indian, and in the years just before her passing, she never talked about it. When I asked questions about my Indian background, she brushed them aside. After she was gone, I tried to research my ancestry. But the court-house that housed Mom's records had burned down. I was left with ashes.

I am a grandmother myself now, and I can look at my own grandmother without bitterness, only pity. I now know that the greatest sadness was all the love she missed. I often reflect on how painful it is when your own family cannot accept differences in people. But a positive legacy has come to me from this experience. I care for all people.

TURN THE
OTHER CHEEK

Rory Elder, Choctow

My grandmother was Choctow and used to talk about her family walking the Trail of Tears from Mississippi to Oklahoma. She told the story to let me know how tough the world can be. She also told it to help me feel pride in being Indian.

Grandmother called me by my Indian name, Nitatohbi —White Bear. She was a great big Indian woman, weighing around 250 pounds. When she squeezed me, which she often did, I felt like a tube of toothpaste. She would squeeze me so hard, with so much love, that I felt as if all my insides would come out. She had a joyous, happy laugh that started way down inside her and rolled out.

We had moved from Oklahoma to Los Angeles when I was just a small boy, and each day Grandmother would pick me up at school and walk me home. She would ask me about my day and then, as we walked, she'd tell stories. It was what I call heart-felt learning. Into all her stories she would weave in a lesson or message that related to my day. To make her point, she pointed to trees, flowers, birds and animals. She found these things effortlessly. It was as if she had a third eye or a special magnet for the things of nature. This was quite amazing to me, as we were in the middle of L.A. "When you are connected," she explained, "you will find these things even in the midst of concrete."

The greatest lesson she taught me was one that was so profound that it exists in me today in what I call a cellular connection—it is literally part of my body.

It happened one day on the way home from school. A group of teenagers began to taunt Grandmother with Indian war whoops. "Where's your tomahawk and feathers?" they jeered at her. She tightened her grip on my hand and walked a little faster, but gave no other indication that she knew they were there.

Then to my horror and disbelief, one of the boys spit in her face. Even with the spit running down her cheek, my grandmother did nothing. She did not wipe the spit from her face as we continued home; she seemed oblivious to it.

When we got home, I was still stunned and shaken at what I had seen done to my grandmother. It was then that she sat me down and talked about what had happened. As I faced her, I could see that there was still a spot on her cheek, but the spit had evaporated.

"There are people in this world who will never know or understand our ways. It is important that you know who you are and be proud of that. I know you wonder why I didn't wipe the spit off. I left it there so you would see that it will dry up, but also so you would know that your heart never will."

As an old woman, my grandmother had a face that looked like leather, with deep wrinkles running through it. But when I looked at her, I saw a story in every wrinkled line. Each wrinkle was a river of wisdom. I would touch her face, and it felt so different from how it looked. It was as soft and warm as her hugs.

Grandmother died at the age of 94. She suffered with Alzheimer's disease in her later years and was in another world much of the time. I flew back to see her shortly before her death and took my nine-month-old son.

When I knelt at her bedside, the spirits chose to give me a special gift. I experienced five minutes of complete lucidity and understanding from my grandmother.

"Grandmother," I whispered in her ear, "I'm here."

"Nitatohbi, you're here," she said, her beautiful old face cracking into hundreds of smile lines.

"Grandmother, I've brought my son to meet you." Her arms reached out to squeeze him like a tube of toothpaste. In these lucid moments she knew that the circle of life had moved my son to her. We sat together, we three, complete in our circle.

She died, I believe, in great peace.

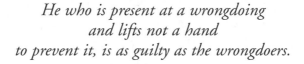

*He who is present at a wrongdoing
and lifts not a hand
to prevent it, is as guilty as the wrongdoers.*

—ESTAMAZA, OMAHA

The Yani Indian Ishi, America's last Stone Age Indian, stepped out of his pre-history world in 1911 to be confronted with a startling, exciting, bewildering new world.

On his death, five years later, his friend Dr. Saxton Pope said:

He looked upon us as sophisticated children
—smart, but not wise.

We knew many things, and much that is false.

He knew nature, which is always true.

His were the qualities of character that last forever.

He was kind; he had courage and self-restraint,
and though all had been taken from him,
there was no bitterness in his heart.

His soul was that of a child, his
mind that of a philosopher.

—Dr. Saxton Pope

FROM THE PERSPECTIVE OF AGE

Bertha Nye Norton, Wintun/Maidu

Ishi liked music. He was always barefooted, and he'd keep time with his foot. There was a brother and sister related to Ishi, cousins I think, who played the guitar for him. Every so often Ishi would come down, traveling at night with his dog, and see them.

I remember and know a lot because I was born in 1899. But there's a lot I've forgotten, too. I've been asking different people about this or that, but everybody is too young to remember. They're all in their 70s.

My great-great-grandfather Pamlo could foresee the future. Many years ago he spoke of the future to me in his ancient Maidu native tongue. He said, "Someday you'll see people fly like geese. One goose is the leader and breaks the air for the rest." Today, aviators fly that same way in formation.

Pamlo also foretold television. One time he pointed to a large wooden cracker box, about the size of a television, the kind we used to have in a general store, and said to me, "One of these days you'll see a man walking around in there, and you'll hear him talking, too." I remember Pamlo didn't care much for doctors. He said nobody could copy the Creator.

Things were different in my youth than they are now. One time a Maidu woman took me up in the mountains. We dug into the ground under the pine trees looking for yellow jackets. Not many people today eat them, but this woman searched them out for food. The yellow jacket combs looked like plates stacked together. When we got back to the village, she put the jacket combs in the fire, browned and salted them, and we ate the yellow jackets and the larvae. I wasn't so very sure I wanted any, but actually it was like eating salted crackers.

I loved to watch my dad dance in the roundhouse. All the dancers would come out and there was nothing more beautiful. There was a big pole in the middle of the roundhouse and each dancer would bless the different directions with clapper sticks.

In those days we threw beads at the dancers to show appreciation. Everyone showed their joy by crying happy tears. I cried too, but I didn't know why I was crying. My mother would laugh, hug me and say, "You're just a little monkey." Today, people throw pennies instead of beads and no one cries. They just clap. I liked the old ways, being a little monkey and crying.

I went to Indian school. I was terribly homesick. A woman gave me a doll, but I didn't want it. I wanted my poppa. In time I got over that, and the doll was with me for quite awhile. I also remember the aluminum combs hurt when they combed my hair.

We went to school a half day. The other half we worked in the kitchen, laundry or sewing room. I worked in the sewing room where we made all of the girls' uniforms. When I had the chance to make what I wanted, I made a little square of lace. It took me almost a year to make it. By the time I finished, the teacher was going to throw it out because it was so dirty. But I was relieved when she washed it instead and even put a little ribbon on it.

Certainly my Indian school days formed a lot of the foundation of my life. But it was my father whose thoughts remain with me even in my older years. I can remember him telling me not to make fun of other people. He said when the ball bounces, it bounces back to you.

My father always told me to be myself. But as this old woman looks at herself, I figure I've pushed that one to the limit!

*Even if the heavens were to fall on me,
I want to do what is right. . . . I never
do wrong without a cause.*

—Geronimo, Chiricahua Apache

A TALE OF A TAIL
OF A HORSE

Dennis Chappabitty, Comanche and Chiricahua Apache

Life hangs by a thin thread. Our destiny is like a leaf blown here and there as the winds blow. My life, and lives stretching two generations back, all hang on the tail of a horse.

I am Comanche and Chiricahua Apache, and my story stretches back to my Apache great-grandfather, James Nicholas (Nico pas, in the original Apache). My mother, Evangelina, had the benefit of being raised as a young girl around well-seasoned Apaches who had actually fought against cavalry and ridden with Geronimo in battle.

In many cases, as the Apache people moved about to evade the cavalry, they were surprised by troops. When caught in the canyons and wilds of present-day Arizona, the Apache warriors always made sure the young and the elderly were spirited out and safe.

This is a tale of destiny, a tale about the tail of a horse as related by Talbot Gooday, an old Apache who actually observed the event. He told the story to my mother when she was a young girl.

Settle down and give me your attention. The story you are about to hear will give you pause for many days to come. It will cause you to wonder about the roads of your past— and how a bend in the path might alter your very existence.

James Nicholas was a noted runner for renegade bands who had grouped around Geronimo in the 1880s. They had gathered to escape the miserable conditions on reservations, where they had been forced to settle. The bands chafed under the corruption of federal bureaucrats responsible for their care and custody. James, who was in his mid-teens, ran miles and miles in a single day, carrying information from one band to another so that the cavalry's position would be known.

On one occasion, the inevitable happened, and as the elderly and children were being escorted to safety, a group of warriors formed a rear-guard action in close quarters with the cavalry, diverting attention away from the escapees. They did this knowing full well that they could be killed or captured. But that was the risk they assumed, to make sure the tribe's people would get away with their lives.

Gooday made it to the top of a mesa, out of reach of the cavalry, and looked down, waiting as the battle continued to develop in the arroyos, with both sides suffering death and casualties. There were bullets flying, and there was screaming, brutality and smoke in the air. No one could see very far. In the midst of hand-to-hand combat, James was fighting a valiant but losing battle. The cavalry was steadily but surely closing in on him and several other young warriors. Gooday figured he could write them off. There was no way any of them could get out.

Suddenly, through the dense gunpowder smoke, another Apache warrior on horseback bolted through the chaos of soldiers and Indians. For a split second the horse and rider went by the place were James stood fighting for his life. James grabbed the tail of the horse ridden by the warrior.

Gooday described James as holding tight to the tail and skipping behind the horse at a full run, with his Apache boots just barely touching the ground between jumps. He literally held on for dear life.

Over a hundred years ago an event occurred in such a flash of history that I could either be here telling the story, or not be here. It is quite staggering to wonder what would have happened if James had missed the tail. Or if his legs weren't in the incredible shape they were from long-distance running.

In modern life, I deal with certain adversities, and things happen that I think are bad. But I think back to James Nicholas, and I know my adversities are small in comparison to past things that have happened to my people in their efforts just to survive.

My existence is tied to a young warrior who grabbed the tail of a horse. I know I'm here for a reason. I'm an attorney, and I help native people defend their rights and get a small degree of justice.

When James got away, he was able to find his way up to Gooday on the mesa. After a short time, Gooday said, "We thought you were lost." James said nothing and continued to move young and old on their way.

James Nicholas is buried in San Carlos Apache Reservation, Arizona. He passed away in the 1930s, a veteran scout for the same military that tried to kill him.

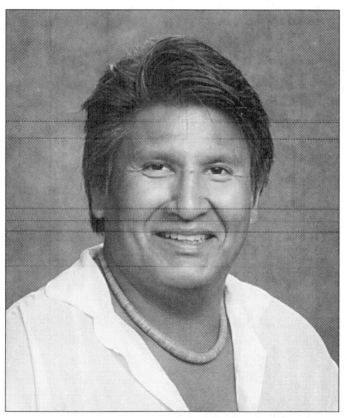

James Nicholas

Every struggle, whether won or lost,
strengthens us for the
next to come.

It is not good for people to have an easy life.
They become weak and inefficient
when they cease to struggle.

Some need a series of defeats before developing
the strength and courage to win a victory.

—VICTORIO, MIMBRES APACHE

ROCK TO ROCK

Santiago Tafoya, New Mexico Pueblo Indian

When I think of all the time I've spent in prison, it seems pretty incredible that it all started with a Buck Rogers gun and a Gene Autry outfit—or was it Hop-along Cassidy? I've forgotten.

I was seven years old when my brother, who was a year younger, and I decided to break into a local drugstore in Leadville, Colorado, where we lived, and swipe the gun and outfit. Why? Who knows now. Seemed to make sense at the time.

My mother had married young and was, admittedly, not very stable. My grandmother once threw hot water on me in a fit of rage, and I screamed like a coyote. That effectively cut off communication between us as far as I was concerned. I remember once intervening when my uncle was hitting my mother. I bit him on the leg. It turned into a free-for-all.

These are sad memories, but then those were sad times for a lot of Americans. The Depression had hit. There were

15 children in my family, and we struggled, with Dad working in the slag mines. Indians were treated really badly, and my mother refused to talk about our heritage. To this day, all I know is that I am from a New Mexico Pueblo group. But I also know that what really counts is the spirit.

When we broke into the drugstore, not only were the gun and outfit there, but my brother got all carried away with jewelry that had silver dollars on it. Then I saw the safe, which was standing wide open. We didn't know until sometime later that the four shopping bags full of stuff we took had $28,000 in them.

I ended up in reformatory school in Golden with my brother. That was my first visit to the rock. The first time I ever took a shower in my life was there, and I was severely beaten because I was afraid of it. I had never seen water coming out of a wall. I was sentenced to be there until I was 21. I escaped 13 times, the last time winding up in California.

There was one stretch, when I was in Buena Vista Reformatory School for five years, that I signed a paper saying that I would box for them. Every time I boxed, 30 days came off my sentence. I ended up winning the Colorado Golden Gloves and dropped my sentence to one year. But I didn't like boxing. It made me feel mean and not good about myself. My spirit certainly wasn't in that. My spirit wasn't in anything.

We could take up a lot of time here going through the next 30 years of my life. I was in and out of San Quentin, Vacaville, Soledad and the Nebraska State Prison. In between, I smoked dope, drank, burglarized and even went back in for not meeting my child support; along the way, I had married and divorced.

On June 11, 1968, at 9:00 am, I was released from the Nebraska State Prison. The warden told me I would get $50 and either a horse and saddle or a bus ride back to my hometown. I took the latter and ended up in Roseville, California, where my family was by then.

My pattern was to jump right back into trouble. But this was the turning point in my life. I met and married a good woman, Janice, who is still my wife. Then an incredible conversation took place at this time between me and—well, when I first heard the voice, I didn't know either.

"Santiago!" I heard my name called three separate times, but when I looked around for the speaker, I couldn't find anyone.

At the fourth call, I said, "What?"

"Are you tired of living this life?"

"Who is this?"

"This is Jesus, the Christ." It was at this moment that I truly saw what I was. The wrongs I had done, the careless, unthinking way I lived. It all started so early that I don't think I ever truly realized how wrong I was.

The same thing happened a short time later while I was asleep.

"Wake up, Santiago."

This time, when I was questioned and got into a conversation, I told the voice that I needed a job.

"See this mountain? I want you to carve it." There in my dream was a mountain, but the message made no sense.

A few days later I was driving around, and there was that same mountain. I went up to the man who owned it, a guy by the name of Wild Bill McCabe, and he gave me a 20-

pound piece of stone from the mountain. I brought it home and tried to carve it. In frustration at not being able to carve it, I finally picked it up and hurled it away. It lay in the grass for a couple months, until one day I was mowing the lawn and hit the rock with the mower. I saw that mountain all over again. So I picked it up, put the mower away and took the rock to a table.

"You said for me to carve this rock, and I told you I don't know how," I yelled out. But as I talked about my frustration, I suddenly realized that I was carving the stone. Before I realized, it was done. All carved. That stone became the sculpture of a pregnant woman that I called "The Last of Her Tribe." Symbolically, I was saying that this was the last of the life I had led.

I have been carving since 1969. Before I start carving, I will wait for the picture to pop into my head. I am in charge of the stone, and I know what will go into the stone. Once in awhile, the stone will break. But it costs $2 a pound, and I hate to throw it away. So I make something different happen. A face will take a different turn, a head will go up or a chin down. All of a sudden, it comes out even better than I had planned.

I work hard in this life for what I have now, and I am happy. I am successful, but I don't want a lot of money. Money and greed were the downfall of my life before, and I want nothing to do with them ever again.

The rock is my friend, my inspiration, my salvation. But I consider Jesus to be the true rock in my life. He is chipping away at me, just like I chip away at my carvings, to make me the human being that he and I would like me to be.

"Woman in the Market Place" by Santiago Tafoya.

SEEKING THE LIGHT

Nathan Windwalker, Cheyenne

Plant a seed. Do not water it or care for it. If it manages to grow at all, it will be withered and ill. I, like that seed, managed to grow, but in a twisted, strange way.

When I was a small child and wet my bed, my mother would put the wet underwear over my head and make me sit in front of the window so my friends could see me.

Years later, when I did work in child psychology, I knew the total depravity of that action. I was abused, isolated and shamed. I was in foster homes, ran away at 12, experienced marijuana, drugs and sex-without-meaning very early. By the time I was 16, I packed a gun, belonged to a motorcycle gang (my "replacement family") and had a massive chip on my shoulder.

One of the few releases and joys in life to me was running. As I ran, I heard drum beats—perhaps my forefathers letting me know they were always with me, and signaling to me of a better life to come.

This withered plant ended up in reformatory school and eventually San Quentin. It was hell. It was in prison that I began to do hospice work. I held men's hands while they were dying. It made me think. I was in the Second Chance program, where I worked with high-risk kids already in trouble, with the hope of turning kids away from prison.

It was about this time that I began to piece my Cheyenne heritage together through the archives of the Church of Jesus Christ of Latter-Day Saints. I did research on my own on different tribal groups and started to see the thread of spirituality that was, in time, to guide my life.

My work with troubled young people in Second Chance tugged at me after my release. That and the hospice work had brought great peace to my soul because I was experiencing service, a giving to others. I now feel that is my path in life.

I do Self-Esteem counseling in schools and work with troubled youths, sharing my past. I tell them that I am now a teacher, but I was once just like them. I use the Native American thinking to stimulate them: family tradition and sharing with each other. We do traditional ceremonies together.

I'm a deep vessel now. I teach affirmative healing in a group of 70 people from all walks of life who gather regularly to experience growth and success in a sharing way. I tell them that by breathing air together, we are all related. That's the spirit of native thinking.

As water and life-giving nutrients seep to my roots, as I am cared for by those around me, the plant that I am grows upward and seeks light.

I will not lie to you.
I do not deceive you.
I come to lead.

—COCHISE, CHIRICAHUA APACHE

In you, as in all men, are natural powers.
You have a will. Learn to use it.
Make it work for you.
Sharpen your senses as you sharpen your knife. . . .
We can give you nothing. You already possess
everything necessary to become great.

—LEGENDARY DWARF CHIEF, CROW

OLYMPIC GOLD

Billy Mills, Lakota Sioux

My life began on the wind-blown plains of South Dakota, where the trees and grass are in constant motion. It was the silence when the wind stopped, which it rarely did, that seemed strange to me.

Maybe the constant motion of the wind transferred somehow to my legs. Maybe it was the wind behind my back that made this Lakota boy a runner. Whatever it was that took me eventually to Olympic competition, in a land far from the Sioux Pine Ridge Reservation, it was a journey that I took for my family, for the people who gave me strength along the way, for Indian people, for my country—and for my dad.

My dad, Sidney, became father and mother to 13 of us when my mother died. I was seven years old. We were very poor, but I never remember my life that way because my father made each of us feel so special. When I think of a way to describe our life on the reservation, the word "innocent" comes to mind. We truly lived a simple, uncomplicated life. It was a healthy upbringing.

My father set the stage for my life. I lost him when I was 12, but before that happened, he taught me what true success is. I have built my life on his words. He showed me a poem by a man whose name I thought was Anonymous. I've learned that it really doesn't matter where that quote came from. It was my dad that made it real for me and helped me in my earliest years to live it.

Success, he said, meant finding positive desires in your life. Desire provides self-motivation. Once motivated, a person wants to work, and with work comes success. Simple. I explored that idea as a young boy, and throughout my life, as I have touched simple people, near-great people, and great people, I have expanded my father's philosophy.

His formula taught me that running was my true desire. That desire unleashed true passion. As I ran the hills and plains of South Dakota, I found that the passion in my legs and soul provided a self-motivation and drive to work that would take me through life. That passion allowed me to acknowledge defeat, too: the races I didn't win, the times when my legs and lungs hurt so badly and my spirit was crushed.

It is that early lesson from my father that caused me to search for and find the gold. From the pursuit of excellence comes victory. My victory in Japan in 1964, as I felt the Olympic tape across my chest, was both a legacy from and a salute to my father: desire, passion, self-motivation, work and victory.

My father had always stressed three beliefs of vital

importance, he felt, to anybody: belief in the Creator (and he did not limit that to any one concept), belief in education and belief in family. After my father's death, his belief in his own family was fulfilled. My older brother Sidney and sister Margie took over our family. My father's belief in education was part of my life. I went to an Indian boarding school in Pine Ridge and eventually on to Haskell Indian School in Kansas. During the summers I would work from 6:00 in the morning until 6:00 at night in Valentine, Nebraska, building grain elevators.

My buddy and I couldn't find a place to stay in Valentine because no one would rent to Indians. So for one month, we found quarters in an old car lot. I slept in the back seat of a Cadillac and my buddy slept in a Hudson Hornet. A creek running nearby gave us baths.

Back in the days when my father talked to me, he always said that desires could be found in drama, sports, music, the arts, reading, writing—anything constructive and fulfilling. He said to me even then, "Billy, I hope you try sports."

When I entered Haskell, where we worked two hours a day for our room and board, that's exactly what I did because the school had an excellent sports program. I knew my decision about sports was right when Coach Tony Coffin stepped up to the mike and talked about intramural sports and league competition. It was at that point that the hair stood up on the back of my neck; Coach Coffin told us that there were three things important to those of us at Haskell: a belief in Creator, education and family.

Haskell felt like home immediately. "We have a history of great athletes, great sports teams, and most important,"

Coach Coffin told us, "great sportsmanship, even beyond the team. Our individual conduct is with character and pride because that's how Indian people are."

I remember him looking out at us, and his eyes settling on me and on Carl Pierce, a Mohawk, the smallest man there, whom we had dubbed "Monster." I was the second smallest person. "I'm not talking to just the big athletes. Who knows. One of you little guys may be one of our greatest athletes."

I wanted to play football. Coach wanted me to run cross-country, but those were my macho days, and I dismissed running as a "silly sport," even though I had done it all my life on the South Dakota plains. Coach told me they needed one more runner for their undefeated state championship team. I still wanted to play football.

I practiced with the football team for three weeks, and even though they were ever so gentle, I was beat up from head to toe. So I went back to Coach. It was time to change sports.

"You were our worst prospect in football," he said. "I was just praying you'd come back to running. Leo Peters holds the Haskell record in the one-mile. I would shoot for his record."

Peters would run 11 miles around Blue Mountain when he trained, so the first day of practice and for the first four days, I ran 11 miles around Blue Mountain. My legs were so tight I couldn't walk. Finally Coach Coffin took me aside and toned me down a bit. The desire that turns to passion had become a bit too passionate.

I came out of high school ranked Number 1 in cross-country and Number 5 in the mile. When I moved on to the University of Kansas, I was not prepared for the rejection I experienced as an Indian. I was not allowed to join a fraternity.

People made fun of Indian names when I talked about my relatives. It became too much after a time, and as a junior, I decided to quit. I found my way to the bus station and called my high school coach to tell him I was leaving. Over the phone, Coach Coffin could hear the announcement that the bus was delayed. A short time later, Tony Coffin walked into the bus station.

I started talking to the coach about my pain, and strange as it was to me to see a grown man cry, he started crying. I thought he felt sorry for the emotional abuse I had suffered.

"Billy," he said, "I'm not crying because I feel sorry for you. I'm crying because you are running away. Most people never find something they can be great in, much less enjoy. That's why I'm crying."

The bus pulled off *without* me and *with* all my bags and clothes. Coach Coffin bought me a jacket and enough Levis and shirts to get by until my bags came back.

In my senior year at the University of Kansas, I married my wife, Patricia, who is still my partner in life. We were moving together toward an incredible journey that would take us to the 1964 Olympics in Japan. It is always surprising to me that people considered my gold medal win an upset. By the time of the U.S. National Championships, Division 1, cross-country, only one American had ever beat me.

I need to talk about a strange thing that happened to me during the period of time I was winning major competitions. I will not comment on why this happened. It is something people will have to decide for themselves. On three different occasions, I was asked to step out of championship pictures documenting the runners finishing in the top slots.

At the National Collegiate Athletic Association (NCAA), Division 1, cross-country competitions in 1960 at Michigan State, I was asked to step away from the camera when the first team, all-American, was photographed. I was devastated. It happened a year later, in the same competition. Many of the athletes were from other countries, attending American schools, and when I was asked to move out of the pictures, a Canadian stepped forward.

"This is your only American winner," he said. "Why are you doing this?"

The final time this occurred was in the Amateur Athlete Union competition, which took place in 1963 in Van Courtland Park, New York. This competition is open to any athlete asked to compete, collegiate or non-collegiate. I was representing the Marine Corps. This time, they hadn't counted on the U.S. Marines!

When I was asked to step aside, after having finished third in the cross-country championship race, the highest American ranked, the photographer was confronted by a Marine Corps officer.

"Lieutenant Mills will not step out of the picture," the photographer was informed. "He is a Marine Corps officer." To make sure there was a complete understanding of the message, the officer proceeded to shake him. I got my picture taken.

It was in Tokyo in 1964 that all the training and teaching I'd received from my dad and my coach finally led me to the understanding that I was not competing against other runners, but against myself. That took tremendous pressure off me.

I had been challenged by these two men from my earliest years to live my life like a warrior. Warriors are both male and female and come from all races. The challenge of the warrior is this:

- To assume self-responsibility and as it is acquired, to reach out and attempt to help others.
- To be humble to all creation—no better, no less than all living things.
- To learn the power of giving: the first thing you can give is respect to yourself, and respect to others follows.
- To be spiritual, allowing humility, giving and self-respect be the core around which to build spirituality.

These were the true challenges I had faced in my life as a warrior. To run for the gold was only an extension of these things.

We had to go to the Adidas store to get our shoes. These would be the first pair of shoes I ever owned that would be my own. When I arrived for my shoes, I was told that there was a short supply of my size and they were holding them for potential winners. The Adidas man escorted me out. I went back in.

"But I think I'm going to win," I said.

"That's a bunch of bull," he responded.

At Puma, I got a pair of shoes. That evening the owner of Adidas came over, apologized and gave me a half dozen pairs of shoes. So it was, in the moments before the race, I was trying to decide which shoes to wear. I weighed them in my hands. Which was the lightest? I decided on an Adidas pair—but history should record that I wore a Puma pair to the victory stand.

After deciding on my shoes, I was the last person out on the track. I looked up to find Patricia in the stands, and then it was time to focus. The field that day was considered the greatest field of distance runners ever assembled for the 10,000-kilometer run. My focus on that event began many months before the race. In my workout books, written months before, was a notation I made:

28 minutes, 25 seconds. God has given me the ability. The rest is up to me. Believe, believe, believe.

When the gold came to me, I had completed my run in 28 minutes, 24.4 seconds.

At the three-mile mark, I was within one second of my fastest three-mile ever, but there were over three miles left and I was only in fourth place. I focused. I thought about Patricia and could see her cheering. I forgot about the others and went back to self-competition. Patricia and I had a dream. We had a goal. We were pursuing it.

With two laps to go, I moved into second place. Four runners remained in the race. Australian Ron Clark, my primary competitor, looked back, saw me and seemed surprised. Later he said about that look back, "At that point, I thought I had won the race." I interpreted that look back to mean that he was worried about the one lap to go.

For a couple of years I had visualized that last lap, being on the lead man's shoulder, springing past him at the finish and breaking the tape. I had for eight months visualized Clark dozens of times a day.

At one point some three months before, my Camp Pendleton Marine coach, Tommy Thompson, had questioned me about the possibility of it not being Clark whose shoulder I would be shadowing. From then on I visualized different competitors. But in the actual Olympics, at this moment, it was Clark.

The rest of the race is history. I was boxed in, managed to pull clear, twice was knocked off balance and had to pull myself back. My visualization of winning was operating at 100 percent. With 30 yards to go, my thoughts were crystal clear.

I felt the tape and knew I had won. I had won! A Japanese official was shaking me. "Who are you, who are you?"

When I was asked what I wanted, I said I wanted a victory lap. But the track was still active. We had lapped one runner three times. He was injured. The Olympic code would not allow a detraction from his integrity. The purpose of the games is not to win but to perform. It was a fitting way for my gold medal to be celebrated. It was in the spirit of my father and my coach.

Billy Mills, Lakota Sioux, winning his
1964 Olympic gold medal in Tokyo, in the 10,000 km run.

TO RUN

Mo Smith, Chiricahua Apache/Navajo
Clan: Hashk' aa hadzodi (yucca fruit strung out in a line)

In her youth, my mother was up early in the morning and out herding the sheep. Navajo land is a land of extremes, very hot and very cold, and the walks were long for her. She was one of 12 children. Her bloodline was Navajo, and she spoke the Navajo language.

My inspiration in life came from this woman, who each morning disciplined herself by running to greet the new day. When she was nearly 12, she went to the Tolani Lake Indian Boarding School, Arizona, and later to Ft. Wingate Indian Boarding School in New Mexico. She went reluctantly, had her hair cut and her hands slapped on occasion. The Navajo language was forbidden. She was an accelerated learner, graduated early and went to Ft. Lewis College in Durango, Colorado. She met my father there, and I was born in Durango.

She was the only one in her family to leave the reservation

because she chose to live away from the reservation and marry outside the Navajo (my father was African-American), there were some Navajo people who made her feel uncomfortable.

My father was an alcoholic, and she had the responsibility of raising a family of five. Poor is a hard word to define. Certainly we weren't poverty-stricken, but sometimes when we were younger, things were tough. There were times, I have to admit, when I didn't have shoes that fit; they were often as much as two sizes too small. My mother had both a day and a night job and often walked four or five miles home from work. I love my mom for what she endured.

Running became my life. She gave me the inspiration to be relentless, to constantly push myself. In high school and college, kids complained about running, and I would think of my mother herding sheep in 110-degree weather and walking long distances home in the dark.

Although my mixed blood may be a little different from mainstream America's, I have always been proud of my heritage. Lack of a good reading background, living in a dysfunctional home and having a father who was never around slowed my way in school. I went to six colleges before I got my degree. That same year, 1986, I ran the mile in under four minutes. As far as I know, I am the only American Indian to have done that.

Running is my heritage. My mother's father, Ralph Paddock, was a distance runner. Slim Whiskers, his father and my great-grandfather, was also a runner. One of our great family stories is about how my grandmother, as she was making stew, needed salt and sent my grandfather to get some. He took a sheep hide, draped it over his shoulders and took off running for the trading post, which was many miles away. The family legend is that before the stew was done, he was back with the salt.

I still picture my grandfather with his old straw hat, doing chores and raking the sand. When you have no grass in your front yard in the desert, you groom the sand. I also had a Chiricahua Apache great-grandfather, Jack McCabe (Bael Do he Chisa—One with Guns), who was a horse stuntman on the Navajo Reservation. He trained and rode wild horses. I guess you could say his genes helped create the showman side of me.

I competed in the 1988 Olympic trials, in the men's 1500-meter race, placing fifth, and in the 1992 Olympic trials, only to be tripped while running in the semi-finals. I will compete again. That's the competitive side of me.

Another side of me runs for sheer joy. Running brings everything together as my feet pound: confidence, identity and a connection to the earth.

When I run, I imagine my great-grandfather Slim Whiskers pounding out the miles across the Painted Desert. He lived to be 110 and ran until he was 90. His persistence, along with my grandfather's and mother's, is my heritage.

My family's persistence is my heritage, and it is in our blood to run.

*The Indian believes profoundly in silence—
the sign of a perfect equilibrium.*

*Silence is the absolute poise or balance
of body, mind and spirit.*

*The man who preserves his selfhood is ever calm
and unshaken by the storms of existence. . . .*

*What are the fruits of silence? They are self-control,
true courage or endurance, patience,
dignity and reverence.*

Silence is the cornerstone of character.

—OHIYESA, SANTEE SIOUX

QUIETLY INDIAN

V. Blanchard Singing Eagle,
Potawatomi/Cherokee/Creek/Chitimacha

My grandmother did not slap me upside the head with our tradition. She didn't speak to me in *Nesnabek*, our Potawatomi language. She didn't even take me to powwows.

Instead, Bubba taught me the beauty of Indian ways simply by being herself. She blended and balanced our customs, never emphasizing or isolating just the Indian within us. So I look back with loving nostalgia upon the "little whiles" we shared, when she wove her stories about Raccoon and Opossum, when she shared her words of wisdom on *Kitchi Manitou*, the Great Spirit. I remember the sage constantly burning in our home and still think of her whenever I smell its ancient, cleansing smoke.

I remember Bubba's enormous, creaky old wooden house in the suburbs of Los Angeles. So strong an emphasis did she place on family that when she bought her house, her sisters, brothers, cousins—all the family—bought houses on the same street. In my family, when someone moved, everyone moved! It was the world of the urban Indian, the quiet Indians whose off-reservation worlds are filled with a colorful sea of faces and experiences, those who have been torn away, but who will always hold their true homes deep within their hearts.

My memories are filled with the countless hours of doing beadwork by Bubba's side, of constantly preparing Indian dishes. Our favorite was Chitimacha Okra Gumbo, which she learned how to cook during her younger days in Louisiana. She used an old Indian mortar, a rock with a bowl-shaped indentation carved in the top, to pound, pound, pound her meal to make our cornbread.

But what I remember most about my grandmother was her admonition, "Above all else, balance, my son." Bubba was the living image of balance. This stability that she maintained in her life has profoundly affected the way I now seek balance, whether I am debating on how much curry versus cream to add to my famous "Algonquin Stew," or explaining to a curriculum committee that teaching Black Elk and Silko does not necessarily mean the exclusion of Milton and Shakespeare. This doctrine of balance also shows me how to live with one foot in the Old Ways and one foot in the Modern Age. So I am equally at home at the computer keyboard or inside the sweat lodge.

Now that I am a parent, I most certainly *do* speak the old language to my children. I take them to as many powwows as they can stand. I teach them about seeking balance in their own lives. But I do so quietly, explaining to them that what makes you an Indian is not the roll number you possess, the reservation you come from, or even the language you speak; rather, it is the balance of life you live.

THE LIGHT

Tom Thompson, Delaware-Lenape

There has always been light in my life. I feel a calmness, a sense of tranquillity that has its roots in my Delaware Indian heritage. I have always been able to turn confrontation into a kind of love.

I was born with a light that comes from sources not clearly understood. I arrived in this life with the skill to play keyboard instruments. One evening in the 1940s, at the age of eight, my parents had taken me to visit friends. A Hoffman upright piano sat in the middle of the living room and the man of the house, who was taking piano lessons, offered to play. He played a song called "Bobby Shafto." When he finished and left the piano, I walked up, sat down and played the exact same song. He was not nearly as astonished as my parents—I had never taken a lesson nor touched a piano before in my life. The first time I sat at an organ, barely able to touch the foot pedal, I played "Silent Night," using both keyboards and the pedals. I cannot logically tell you how I was able to do this. I just knew what to do when my fingers touched the keys.

My parents hired a piano teacher at 50 cents a lesson to work with me. As a young boy, I had an after-school job with the Hammond Organ dealer. I would dust the instruments, clean windows and sweep floors in exchange for the privilege of practicing on the instruments. From that first simple job, I grew to become an international organ concert artist for the Hammond Organ Company, playing in thousands of cities throughout the world. The light gave me a head start.

The light has never ceased to move in its mysterious ways in my life. I am a direct descendant of Chief Charles Journeycake of the Delaware Tribe. He was named for the hard, small, biscuit-like bread the Indians carried with them. In the middle 1800s, he became an early-day Baptist minister to his own people. The unusual effect this had on my great-grandfather, his grandson, was that every Sunday he would put on a neatly cleaned and pressed vanilla-colored suit, which my mother called his "white Palm Beach" suit. When the weather was sunny, he would take an old kitchen chair from out of the farmhouse, take his Bible and go sit in the sun and read all afternoon. I now own that tattered Bible, and inside the front cover, I have placed a very old black-and-white photo of Chief Journeycake to remind me of my special heritage.

In early days growing up in Kansas, all my Indian relatives lived in the same general area. We all felt a kinship with each other and with the Delaware Tribe. The Christianity brought to the Delaware by Journeycake differs from the mainstream and has always tugged at me. It embraces the union of Christianity and Indian thought, which brings into play the philosophy of the Delawares, which is similar to that of many Indian groups: a care and concern for all people and the concept of caretaker rather than owner of land. As a child, at large gatherings, individual family lines blurred and there was a feeling of inter-relatedness among us all. This was Christianity as Journeycake passed it on.

I have always felt great metaphysical unity with Jesus. He never owned a piece of land. I see the parallel in his nomadic ways to many indigenous people who move about the land. I see Journeycake and Jesus both traveling about as they spoke, and many who chose to follow did so physically, following from place to place.

The light has defined my role in life. It needs to shine and go wherever in the world it is needed. The light allows unconditional, non-judgmental love. The light in me invites people to experience these things.

Have patience. All things change in due time.
Wishing cannot bring autumn glory
or cause winter to cease.

—GINALY-LI, CHEROKEE

The longer a problem is allowed to exist,
the harder it is to return to peace of mind.

—TWYLAH NITSCH, SENECA

THE MAN WHO SCALPED COLUMBUS

Adam Fortunate Eagle Nordwall,
Pembina band of Chippewa, Red Lake
Reservation, Minnesota.

Columbus Day, 1968, is a day Italians, Indians and Columbus himself, listening from his eternal perch somewhere, will never forget.

A little history first. The Italian-American Federation in the San Francisco Bay area had for many years performed a re-enactment of Columbus Day at the Aquatic Park in San Francisco. In the past, Sea Scouts had been used to represent the Indians greeting Columbus.

Now picture with me, if you will, these young boys with decorated canoes, turkey feathers in hair, Gucci moccasins, and war paint liberally applied, hopping up and down like a bunch of ruptured chickens in their interpretation of a war dance. It should go without saying that this offended several thousand Native American people in the Bay area. (The Relocation Program of 1958 had brought many Indians here.)

After all, when Columbus arrived, he didn't exactly discover uninhabited land. The native people of this country have made great contributions to global good. Just to name one: agricultural products of the American Indian—potatoes, corn, squash, beans, to name a few—are now used worldwide. When Columbus arrived, these and other gifts ,were offered because Indian people are traditionally giving, sharing people. They kindly gave what they had to the arriving visitors from distant shores.

It seemed logical to go to the root of the Columbus Day problem, so on behalf of the United Bay Area Council of American Indian Affairs, Inc., several of us approached the Italian-American Federation. We asked if actual Indians could be used in the re-enactment, our thought being that this would provide an opportunity to educate society. They were open to using Indians from the area, so for two or three years prior to 1968, Indians had been used in the re-enactment of Columbus's arrival in this country.

However, in those years, American Indian people had never been asked to participate in any of the social or civic events that went along with this celebration. This social slight—the fact that Bay area Indian people were not asked to participate in the feast or parade or anything except the re-enactment program—did, I have to admit, grate on us a bit. We were being exploited but not accepted.

In 1968, we decided to change things. In past years, when Columbus arrived with soldiers and flag, I, playing the role of chief, would go down to his ship and welcome him with an embrace. I would lead him to the staging area; Indians would dance; entertain the visitors from Spain and give them food; and then the area would be cleared for Act Two: Columbus returning to the court of Isabella.

On this occasion, the typical welcome went in new directions. Columbus, played by local businessman Joe Cervitto, walked forward as usual to meet me. He was dressed for his traditional role in a costume of tight pantaloons and the whole regalia. The local newspapers had announced that his new costume cost a whopping $400. My own outfit, of course, with beadwork and porcupine hair roach headgear, was worth considerably more than that— But I digress from my story.

I always thought it was a nice part of the re-enactment when Columbus threw himself down and kissed Mother Earth. Of course, then he would stick the flag of Spain in our soil, claiming America for Spain, which I didn't like so well.

In 1968, like all the years before, Columbus stepped toward me, a soldier on each side, looking for the annual Aquatic Park Columbus Day hug. This is where the surprise started for him. As he stepped forward, I stepped back, holding shield and coup stick and motioning with my head at the two swords the soldiers flanking him were holding. He stepped forward again; I stepped back, nodding at the swords and indicating they should be stuck in the sand. The soldiers did that. Then I placed my coup stick on Columbus's shoulder and began to pressure him downward, saying under my breath so only he could hear, "Get down, get down."

Columbus, a.k.a. Joe Cervitto, dropped to his knees with a big grin on his face. At that point Cy Williams, a Chippewa friend, stepped forward with his spear and snatched the page-boy wig from Columbus's head. A couple thousand people had just witnessed what appeared to be a scalping scene; Columbus was mostly bald under that wig.

We did it in humor, and Joe took it well. A black-and-white photograph taken at that moment shows Joe's grin and all the Indians around him grinning, too. The audience, however, was shocked. The Italians were outraged.

My son Adam ran up to the master of ceremonies of the event, Rick Cimimo, radio station KSFO announcer and a friend of ours, and handed him a note to read. This is what I wrote and what Rick read:

If we had known then what we know now, this scalping is what we would have done to the original Columbus. We cannot undo what history has already done to our people. I think it's about time that all peoples that inhabit our hemisphere come together as brothers and sisters.

We helped Columbus to his feet and put his hair piece back on. Other than looking like he had a bad hair day, he was fine. The audience cheered. Coyote, the trickster, would have been proud of his Indian brothers for pulling off such a clever turnabout of history. The Italian-American committee couldn't see the humor of the event. They just didn't get the message we were trying to convey. In fact, they were damned teed off at the Indians' audacity in symbolically scalping their hero.

The next year we were not asked to participate. So we deemed this day to be a national day of Indian mourning and gathered at the other end of the beach. We set up a tepee and issued black armbands to all Indian people who joined us. A whole group of non-Indian supporters also showed up, and we just kept tearing up black cloth for arm bands.

The Italians were definitely upset, and the head of the committee wanted to know our plans. We suggested that we should have a reconciliation. At some point, when things were quiet on the stage, we felt we would like to come forward and get involved with Columbus. The federation had agreed that we would go down the beach to the staging area.

Columbus was on his boat as in years past, but arrived with no Indians greeting him. The scene then switched, as it always did, to Isabella's court. Things looked quiet, so I decided we should start down the beach to the staging area. Now, I am a pipe carrier, a ceremonial leader, and so as an emissary of peace, I lifted my pipe over my head and began walking the two blocks to the staging area with everyone following me.

All of a sudden, the doors under the grandstand and bleachers opened up and out marched a huge number of policemen, walkie-talkies going and watching us like hawks. This was the era of Vietnam protest, Haight-Ashbury, riots, demonstrations, sleep-ins, sit-downs and lie-ins, so this was not so very unusual in 1969.

A line of blue stretched across the beach, blocking us from the staging area.

I wasn't ready for battle. I mean, I was holding the pipe of peace. I started slowing down, not wanting any conflict. I didn't want my tender head bashed in by police officers who appeared ready and eager to do just that. However, Indians behind me continued to press forward. I slowed down, but the force still pushed me onward. A voice to my side whispered in my ear, "Come on, fearless leader, let's go." I was a very reluctant leader at this point, knowing I would find no satisfaction in getting my head pounded. The heels of my moccasins were dug in the sand, carving two grooves as I was pushed down the beach.

I came face-to-face, eyeball-to-eyeball with a police lieutenant. "You will be arrested if you go any farther," he said. Not wishing to avail myself of San Francisco's police hospitality, I turned to the crowd behind me and yelled, "Sit down." They did. So we sat on the beach, with a big blue line serving as a picket fence between us and the stage. We watched as Columbus hustled through the end of the performance and got off the stand.

There was nothing for us to do. When Columbus was safe and sound, the crowd was dispersed, and there was nothing left on the beach but cops, Indians, squawking seagulls and lapping waves. Then the police left. We were left sitting on the beach.

Columbus Day, 1969. A day of infamy. I don't think there were any honors gained in San Francisco that day.

Adam Fortunate Eagle Nordwall
1968, Columbus Day, San Francisco.

THE FALL OF AN INDIAN

Richard Lyman, President Emeritus, Stanford University

We were the Stanford University Indians, and proud of it! Since the 1930s, our mascot had been an American Indian, either as a heroic warrior figure or as a funny little bulb-nosed caricature. It was supposed to be funny.

By the 1970s, when I was president of the university, a Yurok, who worked in Sacramento as a state civil servant during the week, would come to Stanford Stadium dressed in glorious regalia and flowing headdress to regale the crowd with graceful dancing at half-time. The Leland Stanford Junior University Marching Band provided ample rhythms and drum beats. We loved the pageantry and we loved Prince Lightfoot, as he called himself.

But also in the early 1970s, Native American students began to come to Stanford in appreciable numbers, recruited by an administration anxious to include peoples long excluded from the chance for quality higher education. The American Indian students did not appreciate Prince Lightfoot, still less the bulb-nosed caricature. It wasn't long before they were letting us know why. Heroic or comic, the mascot did nothing to educate the public about the real condition of Native Americans on the reservations. On the contrary, the students told us, the mascot and all the hoopla around it had the effect of encouraging the public to forget the appalling facts about poverty, disease, alcoholism, suicide and the rest.

The romantic costume affected by Prince Lightfoot was not authentic, it turned out, nor were his dances. In fact, the dancing incorporated portions of religious ritual in ways that the Indian students found downright sacrilegious. In any case, by what right did we declare a whole ethnic group our mascot, as if they were bulldogs or tigers?

When the students' complaints were made clear, reactions were various and conflicting. The Student Senate, elected by the student body at large, voted to do away with the Indian mascot entirely. At first, as president, I had thought that if we could discourage use of the bulb-nosed caricature, that would be enough. But the Indian students, with the assistance of the campus ombudsman, persuaded me that nothing short of abolition would do.

At no time did the Indian students mount noisy demonstrations, occupy my office or otherwise attempt to coerce us into agreeing with them. But alumni far from campus found that hard to believe in a time when many campuses, Stanford's included, saw lots of noisy protest against the war in Vietnam.

As we acted to abolish the mascot and forbade Prince Lightfoot to continue his highly popular performances, there was a great deal of unhappiness among many football fans and even more nostalgia-ridden Stanford graduates. My mailbag bulged with outraged criticism. I had caved in to militant Indian students and given away a beloved piece of Stanford tradition. One wealthy alumnus began subsidizing individuals to hawk Indian mascot flags and T-shirts, balloons and feathers at the gates of the stadium. Prince Lightfoot, bitterly hurt that his efforts were not appreciated, managed once or twice to get himself smuggled into the stadium and perform in defiance of the ban.

Eventually things calmed down, though for the entire ten years of my presidency, I had to answer angry critics at alumni gatherings wherever I went, and my successors since 1980 have had to do likewise. To this day a right-wing student paper, the *Stanford Review*, editorializes fiercely for the restoration of the mascot.

But the American Indian students are long since a firmly established and most welcome presence at Stanford. I like to think that taking all the flak was worthwhile, for it showed that the university was serious about respecting all of its members. Of that, I am very proud.

The selfish man is lonely, and his untended fire dies.

—Pima man

Free yourself from negative influence. Negative thoughts are the old habits that gnaw at the roots of the soul.

—Moses Shongo, Seneca

DRUM CIRCLE

Varnina McNair, Pit River/Klamath/Modoc

My early years were spent in Klamath Falls, Oregon,
where I lived with my father and brother. My father was an
invalid and seldom left the house. I never really knew where
the money came from that kept us living very comfortably.
Nor did my father ever talk about his Indian background.
But the thing he was most close-mouthed about was my
mother. My father told me she was dead, and I had never
even known who she was.

When my dad died, I was eight years old, and it was so
hard to believe that he wasn't ever coming back. Right after
his death, I spent great parts of the day sitting under my desk
with a blanket over it, a little girl who couldn't accept her
father's death. People rotated through our house, taking care
of my brother and me for a few days at a time, and then
someone else would come.

In his will, my dad had left my brother and me to his sister in San Diego. But the courts said that children can't be willed like money and possessions. One day a woman finally came to take us to live with her. It was a great shock when she told us she was our mother.

I had seen her on and off throughout my life, and she had been passed off to me as a family friend. She had remarried, and by the time I was ten, I had five brothers and sisters. I got up early in the mornings to help get the kids ready for school and fix lunches. We washed clothes in a wringer washer on the back porch. I am a very responsible person now and think that those early days, with so much responsibility, helped make me this way.

I loved the little babies and often cared for them. it made me feel useful and good to be a mom to my brothers and sisters. My stepfather worked through the day and came home in the evenings. Although I was a little afraid of him, I know he must have cared for us because he took on a second job to support us all. He claimed Potawatami ancestry and adopted many of the Indian ways of my mother. When he died, the people couldn't all fit in the church.

My mother and stepfather were not demonstrative in their affection; no one in our family was. In those early years, I turned to my little sisters, and it felt so good to have those babies to hold and cuddle.

Unfortunately, alcoholism was very much a part of my family and my community. I don't like to talk about all the trauma I felt and all the feelings of not knowing what might happen to me. This lack of stability left its scar.

When I grew up, I thought I had left all the trauma in my childhood behind. I had inherited money from my father, and I went to college. I was at that point a model student. Even though my brother always stayed in touch and was very good to me, he drank too much, and I looked down on him. He died at 18, in an alcohol-related car accident, leaving behind two children. That threw me into a spin. Why had I never acknowledged him for the wonderful person he was? I knew I had bought into someone else's dream of what success was and had turned my back on my family. I was too busy getting ahead. But even though I worked at getting ahead, eventually I found the demon alcohol, as my brother and mother had.

Drinking seemed to shadow us all, and although I drank a lot, I never thought I had a problem—the sign of a true alcoholic. One day I said to myself, "I want a life. I don't want to live in a bar anymore." It was this recognition that moved me toward a new life.

I moved to northern California. There, two extraordinary things happened. The first involved the coincidence of meeting a second cousin I didn't know existed. At the time, I was living in Redding, and it was he who folded me under his wing, talked with me about the Pit River culture and showed me for the first time the homeland of the Pit River Indians. Normally a quiet, closed-mouth man, with me he opened up. It was during our long talks that I realized that my life in actuality had deep roots. I also had glimmers of how my life could stretch in positive ways into the future.

Through him I saw how a family community could work. He had a large, extended family, and whatever was needed by a family member was a group concern. When his mother needed a car, he got her one. I saw and remembered that when you go into an Indian community, people take you in if you need help, even if you are not Indian. There is always food, and you had better be ready to eat wherever you go.

The second thing that happened involved women. By this time I had relocated to the Sierra foothills. What love and stability I had experienced in my life had always come from men. I had seldom looked to women as models. So when at a Maidu gathering I heard a women's drumming group, I was drawn for the first time to a group of women. At a time when I was confused and, I realize now, looking for something to hold onto, the beat of the drum drew me and found an echo inside of me.

I joined the drum group, and it provides a sanctuary for me—to sit in a circle around the drum and see the ring of Indian women faces mirroring mine; to know that others in the drum circle have had their struggles too; to feel the warmth of hugs and caring.

Our drumming and singing is a spiritual adventure and when we sing, something happens to me, to all of us. I feel our ancestors, maybe the ones my second cousin told me about, come to help me sing. I feel humbled and honored and connected every time we drum and sing. There is an energy present that doesn't exist any other place in my life. My circle is complete.

BACK TO THE BLANKET

Victoria Clearwater, Choctaw

I wish my story were a great one about how my grandmother showed me the traditional ways of finding herbs. Or
maybe of weaving a basket. Or even of telling a story.

Quite simply, I don't have a connection with my past.
Born in Texas and raised in southern California, I was
removed from my home, along with my brother, when I was
four. My mother was an alcoholic and my father an abuser.

I didn't hear drumming, go to powwows or eat Indian
fry-bread. I survived. I moved from one abusive situation to
another until I joined the Marines when I was 18. I was a
lady Marine, and my brother Richard became a Green Beret.

I followed the way of alcohol like those before me. So
did Richard, and he's still there. It wasn't until Sun Valley, in
my early twenties, that I finally heard the drums and knew I
was home. There had been a hole inside me for my whole
life, something missing. It was a hole I couldn't fill with alco-

hol and drugs. The hole was filled when I heard the drums. I've done research and am discovering things about my heritage. Most important, it has been 11 years now that drugs, alcohol and tobacco have been absent from my life.

I feel good. Every time I look out the door and see sunlight and life, my heart sings. I've come back to the blanket.

A brave man dies but once —
cowards are always dying.

—MOANAHONGA, IOWA

One has to face fear or forever run from it.

—HAWK, CROW

THE BOBCAT RUN

Ka-ron-ia-waks (Veronica Smith), Mohawk

I heard the Mohawk language more than I did English as
I was growing up on our reservation in New York state.
When we started going to school and got away from the
Mohawk language, my grandmother was saddened because
she was afraid we'd lose the language. She would always say,
"Ka-ri-waks-sen (It's a shame)."

My grandmother could be meaner than a cat, but I also
remember seeing her candle burning in her room and hearing her speak in Mohawk to her Creator. This has in some
way helped me form a closer relationship with the Creator.
I used to watch her making corn husk rugs. To this day I wish
I'd had my head on a little straighter and could remember
how to make those rugs.

There were eight children in our family. We were a
farming family and we worked hard. We always had plenty
to eat: pork, potatoes and Indian corn soup made with a

special corn resembling hominy. Some of the corn was ground into meal for Indian cornbread, *ka-nah-ta-ra kon-ne*. Mumma was such a good cook that we had no trouble keeping hired hands.

We worked hard all day and then all headed for the river with our soap. The river was our bathtub. In the winter, Mumma would heat kettles of water on the wood-burning stove, then one by one each of us kids would stand in a big pan on the floor so Mama could wash us off.

My mother was raised without a lot of love, and we did not get much affection, either. When I was real little, Mumma would put my socks on and then take my feet in her hands and cuddle them to get them warm. That was her one way of touching and loving me.

Mumma was good at reading tea leaves, too, which was a common practice on our reservation. It was such a fun time for us all. We didn't have electricity, so we'd all sit around the kerosene lamp. Mumma would finish her tea, then turn the cup upside down on the table and let the leaves settle a bit. Finally, with all of us hanging on every word, she would began to sift through the leaves and give us her prophesies. I was pretty young then and maybe didn't know everything that was going on, but it seemed to me that she was right a good part of the time.

She was also good at medicine, and I hardly ever went to the doctor. When I was sick, she would send someone into the woods to get the red branches she used. She would boil those branches, and then I would drink the reddened water. I would sweat and get very hot, but she would be there with cool rags. Next day I would be fine.

Mumma was strict. She was big on being on time. Once I was playing at a neighbor's house when suddenly I realized that it was starting to get dark. Mumma had said, "Be home before dark." Just as I had decided that I better get my tail home, I heard a bobcat crying. If you've ever heard a bobcat, you recognize it right away. I was one scared little girl, but with the bobcat threatening on one end and my mother on the other, I figured I'd be better off with the bobcat. I knew I'd better move fast. Halfway home I heard crackling branches and noise over in the bushes. My hair stood on end and, boy, did I ever run! I had the feeling that something was chasing me, but I never looked back. I felt like I was flying. I arrived home in a mixed state of exhaustion and fear. But Mumma must have had a pretty good day because all I got was a scolding.

To this day, I am a very punctual person and get things done on time.

*Do not judge your neighbor until you walk
two moons in his moccasins.*

—NORTHERN CHEYENNE PROVERB

WOMAN OF THE HEALING HANDS

Sacheen Cruz Littlefeather,
White Mountain Apache/Yaqui

I grew up in tremendous despair, anguish and confusion. The good red road I now walk—the light I feel as I experience the sweat lodge ceremony, the feeling of "us" as I relate to human beings, the sweetness of sage smoke—came late in life.

I was part of the urban scene of the San Francisco Bay area. My mother was white, my father of Apache and Yaqui heritage. He was the product of acutely alcoholic parents who abandoned him. I don't remember him as ever showing feelings for me. The neglect and pain he experienced became my legacy. He abused both my mother and me, and my mother became a silent partner in my abuse. My world was silent because my father was deaf. He and my mother communicated in sign language.

The image of me as a small girl going from door to door begging for food haunts me. Not because I still suffer—I've learned to deal with the pain. But I wish I had the power today to stop this madness, so that another little girl doesn't go through terror and humiliation just to find food.

When I needed food and had to beg from others, my greatest dread was that I would be denied. The knocking at a door would echo in the fearful knocking of my heart. I wish I had the power today to stop another child from feeling that fear.

Abuse for my two sisters and me was constant, never-ending. Because that is all I knew, I thought it was normal. I related to life on those terms. I was beaten about the face and eyes regularly, and I was overwhelmed with humiliation that people could see my secret. I took total responsibility for what was happening to me. I placed blame on myself and felt that I didn't deserve good. I wish I had the power today to stop another child from feeling that guilt.

I was sexually abused by three people as a child: my father, an older man whom I trusted, and a 16-year-old teenager who made a practice of abusing children in our neighborhood. Where I lived, domestic abuse happened regularly behind closed doors. There was much poverty and all the problems that go with it.

The first time I spit up blood, I was terrified. I couldn't draw a deep breath without pain. At the age of 3½ I was diagnosed with tuberculosis, the scourge of Indian people. But TB was my path to another life. An oxygen tent in a hospital became my home for a period of time before my grandparents, my mother's parents, entered my life. From that point on, I was raised in a totally white world. My grandparents resented, perhaps rightfully so, everything about my father.

I moved from the hospital to my grandparents' home, where my grandmother, Marie Barnitz, pumped me full of oatmeal and orange juice as we began to fight the ravages of malnutrition. Teri Lee entered my life, too. The doll had hair that could be combed, and my grandmother and I would comb her hair together. Grandmother made clothes for Teri Lee and me.

I would repay her by using my hands to rub her feet, neck and back. It gave her great relief, and she would often take my small hands and place them on her feet or neck. As a young child, my hands already had the gift of healing.

What my grandparents gave me, important to healthy living for anyone, but especially critical for me, was structure and routine: going to bed and getting up at a certain time and doing chores. I joyfully washed clothes and hung them on the line.

At this point in my life, when someone looked at me, with my darker skin, and asked what I was, I would say, "Catholic." That said something about my whole life. I went to 8:00 Mass and received Communion six days a week and attended a Catholic school. I wore a plaid uniform, little brown oxfords and, up to the fifth grade, a beanie. I wore a green beret after that. We stood up when the nun came in, sat down when she used her clicker and opened our desks when she clicked again.

Older children looking at us would chant, "Kindergarten baby, born in the gravy, wah, wah, wah." Even though we were being teased, I liked it because I enjoyed being identified with a group. My waist-length braids were cut into a Dutch bob with bangs and in the second grade, I got a perm. The Shirley Temple look was in, and I was a darker version of Shirley. It wasn't until high school that I rebelled and went back to my long, straight black hair.

All was not rosy in paradise, however. I was taunted in school because of my color and called "nigger," "pagan," "heathen," "savage" and "blanket ass." Having a Spanish last name caused some people to assume that I was Hispanic, which only added to the confusion. No one remembered that long ago, many Indian groups of the Southwest were conquered by the Spanish and given surnames by the Spanish missionaries.

At nine years of age, I was very overweight and the name "Fatso" was added. A glandular specialist determined a thyroid problem and a strict diet resulted. I dieted with gusto, exercised fanatically and went from 130 to 80 pounds. I noticed people liked me better without weight. I got some sort of respect. I began to feel that if I was 83 pounds rather than 80, I was fat. This was the beginning of my anorexic life.

I began to equate my weight with my self-esteem. I believed the skinnier I was, the more I would be liked. I graduated from high school at 17, thinking myself fat at 5'8" and 117 pounds. By this time I was attempting to communicate with my father. My acceptance at three colleges brought the response from him, "Trying to be better than me, huh?" Those were the words that sank the ship. I wanted him dead and quite frankly, hated his guts.

He did die, shortly thereafter. My mother partially

blamed me for his death because she felt I did not accept or forgive him. When he died, my mother saw a blackbird on a bush outside his window. Blackbird was my mother's nickname for him, and when the blackbird flew into a ray of sunlight, she felt he had crossed to peace.

He didn't have peace in his lifetime. My father had been victimized by his parents, who abandoned him, and because of his deafness he had been forced to learn to talk all over again. He took his rage out on the world. His rage was directed at me, too. It did not end with his death. That was the beginning of a new pain. I had nightmares after he died that he was coming to kill me, and I would wake screaming. Paranoia led to a nervous breakdown and a suicide attempt. I was placed in a psychiatric hospital for long-term care. I was there for one year.

When I came out, I went on to college. Self-esteem was a weight-scale again, and I regularly denied myself food. It was almost as if I wanted to become so thin that I'd disappear.

Life did not get easier as a young woman. My life has been so crazy, even I don't understand it. My first job as a public service director for a radio station brought with it a horrible man who practiced workplace sexual harassment.

It was at this time that I joined a group of young urban Indians, led by traditional elders, on an excursion into the out-of-doors. The transformation in my life began. For the first time, I was identifying with and experiencing the ceremonies and teachings of my native ancestors.

As I first experienced the sweat lodge ceremony, in the darkness and next to the womb of our Earth Mother, I was able to free myself, cry out and let go of my pain. I then joyfully submerged myself with the other Indian women in a deep pond nearby, dried myself and slept peacefully that night.

I listened to the stories of the elders, to their wisdom from which they spoke, and felt a new sense of myself. This feeling broke through my isolation, and it was now "us," "our" and "we."

For a child of darkness, depression and pain, coming to the light of belonging has been a miracle. Prayer helped me through childhood, and I know the Creator listens even in despair, a place I've visited many times in life. A medicine person told me that if you pray for the person you hate and detest, the anger is defused. That's right. I am now free to love my parents again. It is good that the bitterness has gone. Without the bitterness, I have been able to deal with surgery that is now restoring my vision. The facial batterings of my early youth created severe traumatic injury that has almost taken my eyesight.

I am a trained health educator and work in alternative health care and nutrition. I have a bit of knowledge about native medicine in herbs and plants, too. But the true magic is in my hands, those same hands, so little then, that used to rub my grandmother's feet and neck. I am a certified massage therapist.

My hands are those of a healer. As my eyes fail, my hands grow more sensitive and stronger. When I lay my hands on a human being, I know the power is there.

©Ilka Hartman, 1995.

Sacheen Littlefeather, 1971.

Kindness is to use one's will to guard one's speech
and conduct so as not to injure anyone.

—OMAHA ORAL TRADITION

Lose your temper and you lose a friend;
Lie and you lose yourself.

—HOPI PROVERB

To be lazy while there is plenty means
death when there is little.

—WINNEBAGO PROVERB

Do not stop watering the corn while you
count on the clouds to bring rain.

—DAN GEORGE

HUCKLEBERRY MEMORIES

Melissa Campobasso, Colville Confederated Tribe,
Okanogan and San Poil

Christine Williams, my great-grandmother, lived to be well over 100, spoke the native Salish tongue, and because she lived so long, made the transition from the very old and traditional to the contemporary world.

When I think of her, I think of huckleberry pies. She would bake and whip out great numbers of pies for family gatherings, funerals and weddings. Whatever the event, there were always huckleberry pies.

Things were never easy for her, and she saw many changes during her lifetime. Up through the 1930s, the salmon runs provided about half the diet for our Okanogan tribe. My grandmother lived through the period of time when dams like the Grand Coulee were built, which meant the great salmon runs stopped.

The end of salmon fishing, as the tribes along the Columbia River had experienced it for centuries, was one of the steps that caused a great breakdown in the culture of the peoples along the river. I wasn't raised in a powwow family. In other words, I wasn't closely associated with other Indians in the area and, quite frankly, it was by choice.

When I was young, I looked around at the Indian community and saw the drunks, the broken-down cars and dirty yards, and I deliberately hung out with white friends. I had my bad times in a white world. I remember thinking how pretty I thought their light skin was, and I'd hide my brown arms under my desk at school. But I still chose to live in that world.

In high school I started learning more about my people by reading books and talking to other Native Americans. Even though I was Indian, I always thought of Indians as mostly just dancing around fires. I had created a stereotype of my own people. I found that indigenous people were a lot more sophisticated than I had realized. They had established governments, the Iroquois Confederacy as one fine example, and had democratic systems that worked well. Everyone was fed, taken care of and had freedom. That was pretty advanced.

I looked around my own world with different eyes. I began to understand why there were broken-down cars and depressed people. There were few opportunities, no jobs, people not believing they could go anywhere, and few positive media images. I guess what I went through is known as growing up. Some people never do grow up, no matter how old they get, so I am grateful that I took the time to try to understand.

Part of my expansion involved honestly getting to know and experience my great-grandmother, not only as an Indian, but as a woman. She was a strong woman who had been left by her husband. She was illiterate, had no driver's license (always had her kids driving her around), but had remarkable persistence and fortitude. She hired a couple hands and kept the farm going. She kept on even when her own kids and everyone around her died. She outlived most of her own family.

My mother, Ramona, who, incidentally, inherited the persistency that characterized her Grandmother Christine, loves to tell the story of the time she and her grandmother were thinning an apple tree, one on each side. Christine Williams was pretty old at the time, and my mother, who was 16, kept trying to work around the tree and do more than her share to help the older woman. You didn't do that to Christine. The more my mother did, the more Christine did. Here we had two persistent woman ripping apples like crazy off a tree. I am now in line to inherit the persistence of these two stubborn women.

My great-grandmother had only one eye, which made it hard for her to bead. She wore tinted glasses and thought she was ugly. My mother would often reassure her she was not.

In addition to my persistent nature (yes, I did inherit that), I value the lesson my great-grandmother gave my mother when it came to dealing with life and passing on tradition. "Bake a pie," she would say. "When you're feeling down, do something. That's the secret to healthy living. Don't just sit around—clean clothes, take a drive, visit someone, do gardening—because the bad times pass."

She especially stressed keeping a strong relationship with the earth. "Get outside and appreciate the beauty. When you're depressed, it's good to see that other things are still in order. That offers hope and comfort. Let nature be your friend."

Just a few months before she passed into the next life, she stressed that my mother should continue the traditions: "Do sweathouse, pick berries and dig roots—these things are very important." I'm happy to say that I have completed the circle and done my great-grandmother's bidding. My family, including my mother and I, have dug roots and sweated in the same place where Christine sweated along the Okanogan River.

Although she's gone now, I cannot be in the out-of-doors without thinking of her. But most especially, when I smell a huckleberry pie, do I remember Christine Williams.

*The Ute who follows two rabbits will
perhaps catch one, and often none.*

—DAN GEORGE

CREE FAMILY

Joan Beatty, Cree

My parents raised 13 children in an isolated Cree community of 800 in northern Saskatchewan, Canada. Our first
language was Cree and that continues to be the only language we use at home. My mother speaks nothing but Cree,
my father speaks Cree and English. Both read Cree syllabics.

Our main sources of income were trapping in the winter
and commercial fishing in the summer. We spent most of our
time on the trapline in the winter, living in a small log cabin
my father built. For years, he used a team of dogs, traveling
miles every day to check his traps. Sometimes he camped
overnight. Those were scary times, especially when the dogs
started barking at night. We were afraid of wolves.

Each of us had our own traps. My mother helped us set
them. Every day, after our chores were done, we walked a
couple of miles into the bush to check our traps. There was
great anticipation, hoping that instead of a squirrel there

would be a mink. Once, and only once, did I get a mink. I still remember the thrill. My mom did most of the work, preparing the pelt, just as she helped Dad with preparing the skins.

Mom worked side by side with my father all her life. Initially, her role in the family was to take care of children. We never went without a hot meal and clean clothes. Then as we grew older, she began to do things on her own, like getting her own trapping license.

She and Dad are still trapping, even though he's in his 70s and she's not far behind. The only difference now is they can drive the 75 miles to the trapline instead of having to move there. Once they get into the bush, they use a Ski-doo to get around—the snowmobile has replaced the dog team. They each have their own set of traps which they check together.

Throughout my childhood, summer meant fishing camp. Our camp was on a sandy beach by Ballantyne Lake. Mom cooked over the campfire, sometimes using a little stove inside if the weather was bad. Every Saturday we would head into the bush and gather spruce boughs for tent flooring.

I remember one night in particular, when Dad was sitting by the kerosene lamp reading his Cree Bible. A bat flew into the tent. Cree legend says that if a bat pees on your head, you will go bald. The sight of the bat had all of us screaming and covering our heads. Dominating the scene was my dad, who was chasing the bat around, swinging at it with his Cree Bible, trying to get the bat to seek more hospitable quarters.

Again, in fishing as in trapping, my mother became increasingly involved in Dad's work as her mothering responsibilities lessened. It gives me a lot of pride to know that she is the first woman in the Deschambault Lake

Fishermen's Co-operative to get a commercial license. In their older years, my folks have become great buddies, working together with their trapping and fishing. I am always touched when I see my father, who rises at 6:00 A.M., make coffee and take it to my mother in bed. He also makes great sourdough pancakes!

My father is an elder in our community, continuing to advise Indian leaders and governments. For years, he was mayor of our town and responsible for, among other things, bringing in the first store and the first school. He showed us by example what community spirit meant. I remember that my dad encouraged all of us to aim high in life, whether we were boys or girls. He didn't differentiate daughters from sons when it came to setting rabbit snares. What a feeling of warmth it brings to remember being with my dad on the rabbit trail. Even today, one of my favorite foods is rabbit stew.

My mother created in me, as a young child, something that I now know is unusual for a little girl. I wanted to go to bed early! I looked forward to her storytelling and what stories she would tell. Her best stories were always of Wesakeja, the Trickster. My brothers, sisters and I would hang on every word. Sometimes Mom would drift off to sleep in the middle of a story, and we'd prod her and yell, "Ekwa . . . ekwa? (And . . . and?)" The stories were often continued, so we would have to anticipate during the day what might be going to happen next. Nightfall would have us excited and ready for storytelling time.

It's strange about formal education in our family. My parents don't have formal educations because there were no schools in their day. But they passed on to all 13 of us, by sheer example, the value of hard work. We got the education they never had. Today we are teachers, administrators, government policy makers, a police officer, a nurse, a carpenter, business owners and, of course, me, a journalist.

Extended family and community were strong in my upbringing. When my mother spent months in the hospital from an extended bout with poor health, her mother, my Grandma Angelique, became even more important in our lives. Dad used to pitch a tent in the back yard so we could sleep out with Grandma. "Look," she'd exclaim as we watched the Northern Lights flicker across the sky. "The ghosts are dancing."

I spent hours sitting beside her, drinking tea and watching her make birch bark baskets, decorating them with dyed roots and porcupine quills. It was from her I learned patience. She was the only one in the village that made baskets, whittling away at red willow, peeling the roots and collecting birch bark. Sometimes she used the bark off the red willow, scraping it off and boiling it for dying the roots. The roots would come out a beautiful pink and red.

Our family is now scattered throughout the province. There are 45 of us and we are close, gathering frequently for holidays. Often, as I work in my chosen profession, I lose focus and get caught up with the daily realities and stress of deadline. That's when I head for my home in the north, to refocus, but most important, to renew my spirit.

THE ISLETA LIFE

Margaret Jojola, Isleta Pueblo

When I think about things that have always been a part of my life, I think of bread. Our bread, or *bahou* in our native tongue, here at Isleta Pueblo is baked in outside adobe mud ovens that look like teacups turned upside down. I was born in 1918, and as soon as I was old enough to walk and talk, I helped my grandmother make bread.

We make the dough the evening before. We build a fire in the oven, and after it has burned down we sweep the ashes out through the arched opening in the side. Then we mold the dough into round mounds and place it on pans. When I was a girl, we put it directly on the mud floor of the oven. You know, when I look back, the bottom of the bread was always clean and nothing from the floor ever stuck to the bottom. I don't know when we got so particular and fussy and started using aluminum pans.

I own a little shop across the plaza from the church. It is

the same spot that my grandmother had before me when she sold her pottery and bread. When she started selling, she just had her pots sitting outside. My shop today handles all sorts of American Indian arts and crafts that I buy or trade from Navajo, Zuni, Laguna and other nearby Indian groups. I'm a good businesswoman, but please understand that I don't always work eight hours a day. I know how to take time off.

As a little girl, I loved to go with my grandmother to the river to get clay for her pottery. While she'd look for just the right clay, I'd spend my time looking for shiny stones along the river, under the cottonwood trees, to use for polishing her pottery. She had a way of making me a part of her life and her work and giving me a sense of belonging and worth.

Once Grandmother had her clay, she took strips of it, rolled the strips and began to coil them into a pot, using a gourd scraper to even the lines. To fire our pottery, I would go out into the nearby cow pastures with burlap bags and collect cow pies (that's dried manure for people who don't understand). My grandmother and I would put a base of rocks on the ground, place the pottery on it and cover it all with my cow pies. Then the whole pile would be set on fire. When everything cooled, I would dig down and pull out my treasures. The pottery was now red with black markings.

Then there was the rabbit hunt. How I loved the excitement! Now that I'm older, I realize how much community spirit we had then. After two days of dancing, the men would form a large circle some distance from the pueblo. As they walked toward the center of the circle and it became smaller, rabbits started hopping every which way. The men took cottonwood sticks with a ball on the end, took aim and let fly. That would be dinner for the evening. We women rode out on wagons, met the men and ate lunch on the mesa.

It was a world of closely knit people and strong families. People must remember the underlying values that existed then—the simple things in life that made us strong and made life worth living.

*Honor age! Even an old blind man
may guide you to a rainbow.*

—MICMAC PROVERB

JENNIE'S HANDS

Cheewa James, Modoc

My great-great Aunt Jennie's hands were as gnarled and withered as an old oak limb. On Sundays during the early 1940s, my family would visit her, and I sat at her feet as she told stories. Her hands were always at my eye level. At first they frightened me and reminded me of a bird's claws. But Sunday by Sunday, I got used to them. They were part of her.

Jennie Clinton was the last survivor of the Modoc Indian War, fought in northern California in 1872-73. Although the Modoc were sent as POWs to Oklahoma Indian Territory after the war, she had returned to the Klamath Reservation in Oregon soon after the turn of the century.

Jennie often read to us out of the Bible. She was totally blind. Like most of the Modoc, she had become a Quaker after her arrival in Oklahoma. Knowing she was losing her eyesight, she memorized great portions of the Bible. My brother, sister and I would gather at her feet, she would open her Bible to a prescribed page and "read."

Jennie was also a master storyteller in the tradition of American Indian people. Where written language does not exist, passing information down orally becomes an art. Medicinal cures, theology, food gathering techniques—all phases of life were passed down by word of mouth. When survival depends on accuracy, storytelling is an art.

When she was through reading or telling us stories, Jennie opened her old screen door, shuffled into her tiny house, and pulled out an old suitcase from under her bed. We kids piled in behind her because we knew what was in the suitcase. She bought candy at the Williamson River store and kept it there.

Jennie Clinton taught me the beauty of sharing time with words. We have so many substitutes today. People now have no idea how their parents met, what their grandparents did as young people, or even what happened on the day they were born. But there is something even more important than passing information on through our families.

You see, I don't remember a lot of what Jennie said. I was quite small at the time. But when I think of her crackling old voice drifting through the air on those lazy Sundays, I feel a warmth, a flood of human caring. To this day, when I see the bony, aging hands of elderly people, I feel love.

Jennie Clinton, last survivor of the 1872-73 Modoc War.
Great-great niece Cheewa James as a child, author, seated.
Cheewa's brother and sister, Sonny James and Viola James, standing.

SHAWNEE BLOOD

Mary Rainman, Shawnee

My early life did not go well. At the age of 15, having been in and out of trouble, I was attending school on the reservation. I was unhappy, unruly, unladylike and had a mouth—a big one. I finally went too far and was put on probation. Part of my probation included assigned community service.

Things happened then that turned my life around.

My assignment was to help an old Indian woman by the name of Anna every day after school and days I was out of school. On the first day, resentful toward the world, I trudged up the hill to Anna's house, which overlooked our small village, and found her to be everything I'd imagined: baggy old sweater, slipping teeth (which I could hardly stand to watch) and a face so wrinkled it was hard to imagine she'd ever been young.

She asked me to bring in firewood for her ancient iron kitchen stove and to help her fix a meal. Lowering my eyes,

I stomped off to get the wood, leaving no doubt as to what I thought of her and the forced labor. I built her fire, slamming the stove door angrily, then waited for her next order.

It was as if she didn't even sense my dislike of her and her tasks. In her wavering, slow voice, she began to tell me how long she'd been making Indian fry bread and how much she liked it. She began showing me how to knead the dough.

During the evening I split more wood for her, my silence speaking my frustration and hostility. The only good part of the evening was the fry-bread, which was indeed as good as she said it would be. As I jerked my coat from the kitchen chair to leave, she motioned me to lift a sugar bowl off the shelf. She took the cracked lid off and, out of a pile of coins, selected two nickels and held them out to me.

I was startled; working for her was punishment, not something for which I was to be paid. Didn't anyone tell her the rules? I even figured I would get in trouble by taking the money. I shook my head, threw my coat on and let her walk me out the door and across her rickety porch.

"Tomorrow," she said and slipped inside.

Crazy old thing, I thought, and started down the hill. Halfway down the hill, I heard a clinking, reached in my pocket, and found the two nickels. At first I was alarmed. Then I began to wonder if I could keep the school from finding out about the two nickels. After all, she'd pushed the money on me.

The pattern of my life over those next few months was woven together with Anna's. I couldn't believe her patience at my belligerence, which was very planned and purposeful those first few weeks. She often talked of how we shared

Shawnee blood and how grateful she was that someone from her community was there to offer her help and service. That was the old way, she said, when the Shawnee spirit of community was strong. I often wondered if they'd explained why I was really there. Maybe she didn't understand.

She never again offered me money, but the two nickels always were there in my pocket. I was at first very nervous that I'd be found out. But as the days wore on, I came to realize that no one would ever know. It took the sting out of the probation.

One day my principal brought me into his office and said the probation was over. I had shown much improvement, he said. He was proud. My alarm at what would happen to Anna surprised him. He assured me that someone else would surely help her; I had done my part. He never mentioned the money. He obviously didn't know. That evening after school, I didn't go to Anna's house. I went to the general store with my pile of nickels heavy in my pocket.

When I trudged up the hill the next evening, I could see her anxious face looking out the door when she heard me coming. Didn't they tell her it was over with me? Were they just going to let her stand around waiting for me each evening?

We went in the house, and I opened my big package from the general store. I took off her old sweater and placed the new, soft one around her shoulders. Her face told me she'd never allowed herself anything like this before.

Many years have gone by. I don't live on the reservation anymore. I have children of my own—and a husband who thinks I make the greatest fry-bread there is.

And when I talk with my children about the sense of community and caring that I feel life is all about, I think of Anna once again, and how we shared Shawnee blood.

No one likes to be criticized, but criticism
can be something like the desert wind that,
in whipping the tender corn stalks, forces
them to strike their roots down
deeper for security.

—POLINGAYSI QOYAWAYMA, HOPI

Mother Corn has fed you, as she has
fed all Hopi people,
since long, long ago when she was
no larger than my thumb.
Mother Corn is a promise of food and life.
I grind with gratitude for the
richness of our harvest,
not with cross feelings of working too hard.
As I kneel at my grinding stone,
I bow my head in prayer,
thanking the great forces for provision.
I have received much.
I am willing to give much in return . . .
there must be a giving back for what one receives.

—SEVENKA QOYAWAYMA, HOPI

LAND OF ACORNS

Alfred Elgin, Pomo

Life is full of decisions. What seems to be the best decision at the time can have a funny turn at the end.

That quirky sort of decision was made by the Pomo
Indians of the Dry Creek Rancheria, located near
Geyserville, California. People today associate Indians with
reservations, but in California the federal Rancheria Act
back in the 1920s gave small parcels of land to Indians
already living on the land or in the area, rather than putting
aside a large reservation and moving Indians onto it.

My father, Alfred Sr., was just a small boy when our
Pomo group was offered two sites for their rancheria. There
was, as one choice, the bottom land next to the Russian
River—pretty rich land, even today, for crops. The other
choice was 77 acres of rocky, hilly mountain land that didn't
have a level land site on it. Now maybe to an outsider today
looking at the decision, it would appear that the river bot-

tom was by far the best choice. But remember, this was back in the 1920s, and life was different then.

What I didn't tell you was that the mountain land had two things in great abundance: deer and acorns. For someone who's never had acorn soup or mush, known as *tubo* in the Pomo language, it's probably hard to understand why the Pomo picked that harsh mountain land for their rancheria.

Acorns were a staple of the Pomo. They would gather the acorns, break them in half and allow them to dry. Then they would pound them into chunky pieces; that's how they were stored. When it was time to actually use the acorns, the pieces were ground into a fine flour.

But the flour was bitter until it was put on a cloth-bound basket and washed clean! The flour mixture was formed into a round loaf, placed in leaves and buried in the ground with heated stones to make acorn bread.

Time changes things, and the acorn and the deer aren't to the Pomo what they once were. But there's a good moral, I think, in the Pomo story. Before we make a judgment about any decision, we should know all the facts.

The rancheria was closely knit, with seven or eight families living together. My great-grandmother had seven daughters, and all of them lived there for a period of time. When I think of the rancheria, I think of rocks, rattlesnakes and carrying water up the hill.

Contrary to many people's concept of Indian organization, tribalism was not as important as individualism to the Pomo. The Pomo stressed working to earn your own way and being dependent on your own skills and abilities. That was my father's great legacy to me, and he did it by spending time helping me with sports. He managed many baseball teams, and I grew up as a batboy with a bat in my hand. At 13, I was swinging a bat competitively and didn't retire from recreational ball until 42, when my legs wouldn't make it around the bases.

My grandmother, Elizabeth Lozento Dollar, was widowed early. What a woman she was! She was illiterate— could not read or write a word. But during a period of time that she worked for a Catholic priest, she managed to learn fluently or semi-fluently seven different languages, including three or four Pomo dialects.

At one point, she worked for a doctor. One day the doctor became irate and called her an illiterate Indian. She paused for a moment, then asked him a question. He didn't understand the language she was using, so she asked again in another language. And another. Finally she looked at him and said, "You speak only *one* language, and you think I'm illiterate?" He later apologized to her.

No one could ever say that Grandmother did not have spunk. One time, when she felt her second husband was not acting properly, she stuffed him in the trunk of their car until he agreed to behave.

My grandmother gave me my first job, at $1 an hour, as part of her farm crew. This "illiterate Indian woman" by now was running a crew of 15 to 25 people that worked the hop fields. She managed her business competently and fairly. During the Depression, when people lost jobs and were barely scraping by, it is said that she fed practically the whole rancheria.

I remember one time saying that I would have liked to

live in the good old days on the rancheria. "Honey," she replied, "those weren't good old days. Indians weren't respected and they were misused. I had to escort my sisters so they wouldn't be raped. I carried a six-shooter then." She stressed that you have to grow and build on what you have and not worry about the past.

Back in 1928, four years before my birth, my grand-mother was a midwife for a Protestant minister from the Midwest. That contact was to cause her to switch from Catholicism and to put in motion an energy that would affect me. Years later, I became a minister, finding a way to give a service and help to Indian people.

I have in my possession a unique basket with no bottom. It was made by my great-great grandmother and was repaired many times by my grandmother. The basket is designed to be placed over a hollowed out rock or log used for grinding acorns. I also have a round rock that she used to pound acorns. She found it when she was 11 years old, on the beach at the mouth of the Russian River. My grand-mother said it took her grandmother 25 years of pounding to get it into the perfect shape for working the acorns.

What joy it brings me to have these two things from times gone by. When I touch them, I feel again the old tug of the past. But then my grandmother's words come to me, again: grow and build on what you have.

THE ART OF GIVING

Wilson A. Romero, Sr., Cochiti

Most people don't eat robins, but I used to take my sling-shot and bring home robins, ducks and rabbits to eat. Robins are part of the Cochiti diet. They taste like cedar because robins eat cedar berries.

Life at Cochiti Pueblo when I was a boy was kerosene and outhouses. It wasn't until the 1950s that the Public Health Service brought us electricity, running water and sanitary conditions. Life there was also cottonwoods by the river, blue corn tortillas and horse races. My horse was named Red and he loved to jump fences. We were good friends, Red and I, and each morning and evening I would go to feed and water him and the other horses.

There were always horse races at the San Juan fiesta and on other fiesta days throughout the summer at the pueblo. The horse race centered around a chicken or a rooster that was buried loosely in the sand, with only its head sticking up.

The object was to ride by and pluck the chicken from the ground. It was your chicken if you could get it. But plucking the chicken out wasn't easy, and sometimes that chicken was pretty ragged by the time the winner had his prize.

As children, we made many of our own toys. I floated a lot of sardine-can boats. We played the game of shinny stick, which is almost like polo and golf put together, and is played on foot.

My parents worked in Albuquerque, and so life for me centered around my grandparents. We lived off the land, my grandfather hunting and raising all our food and grandmother cooking it. Grandmother was a potter and cooked in pots that she made. If my mouth waters for robin, it also remembers rabbit and chili stew, tamales, wild celery and peas and a wild vegetable we picked, called *cashe* in our Keres language. Cashe multiplied very quickly, and when we went to pick it, it was growing everywhere.

The finest thing about Cochiti was the closeness of all the people. I felt rooted and cared for by everyone there. The community spirit in Cochiti was strong. My grandfather set the model for me. He said, "Always make friends and help people out." When I joined the service, I made friends all over the Pacific. I especially liked Hawaii and got to know Filipinos, Samoans, Puerto Ricans and, of course, the native Hawaiians. Every weekend I would be in somebody's home, always bringing a crate of chickens and rice. They wanted me to stay in Hawaii, but my roots and heart rested in New Mexico with the Cochiti.

As much as my grandfather hammered at me to help people, he also never let me forget how important it was to get an education. I went to the Bureau of Indian Affairs School in Cochiti for my early education, then was bused to Bernalillo High School, a distance of 32 miles, for my middle and high school education.

When I graduated from college, I came back to the reservation and helped establish the Indian Education Program. I also now head the Cochiti Youth Dance Group for young people, who share their talent and culture with those who invite them to perform.

The Cochiti people have given me warmth, caring and a good life. In keeping with my grandfather's strong feeling about giving to others, I am now able to repay my debt to my village. I have brought the gift of education to their children. But it is a special gift of learning. I am teaching them to walk in both worlds.

Wilson A. Romero, Sr., Cochiti, and author Cheewa James.

*We live, we die and, like the grass and trees,
renew ourselves from the soft clods of the grave.*

*Stones crumble and decay, faiths grow old and they
are forgotten, but new beliefs are born.*

*The faith of the villages is dust now, but it
will grow again like the trees.*

—OLD ONE, WANAPUM

FISH PEOPLE

Lavina Brooks, Yurok/Karok

We are the fish people of the Klamath River in California. For generations the Yurok and Karok have lived off the land, swinging their fishing nets out over the river.

Our tribal life is very communal. The fishing that sustains us is a cooperative venture and creates a sense of family belonging. Because we fish at night, everyone has to help. Traditionally, the women keep the fire going, smoke the fish and watch the children. As we have become more limited by the government, however, as to how many nets each person can have, women have begun to work their own nets just like the men.

I am half Indian. My mother, Janet, who is the Indian part of me, had incredible follow-through and thoroughness. When we look at gifts parents give us, we often don't realize the most important until we are older and have a sense of what is needed in life.

When my mother looked at a basket, she wanted to

know who made it. She wanted to know the history of each basket she touched. Perhaps it was this insistence on knowing that made her a master at oral history. She was always accurate and well-organized.

Everything my mother touched was imbued with quality. "When you make a basket," she said, "go where the good basketmakers go. Don't pick just anyplace to get your materials." So I learned that you go to Camp Creek for sticks and toward Bald Hill for bear grass.

It was hard growing up with mixed blood. My mother and her family always loved and accepted me, but in some ways I felt like an outsider because my father was white. Until the Brush Dance.

It was during the Brush Dance that young, unmarried girls, usually 11 or 12, are introduced and dance. In this three-day ceremony, Yurok, Karok, Hoopa and Tolowa come together. This is where everyone meets everyone. It was in my first Brush Dance ceremony that the full reality washed over me: I was a complete part of these people.

That total recognition of my identity has helped me move through life with confidence, constantly working to grow. I have two daughters of my own now, Bessie and Onna Joseph. Both of them will be graduating soon from college. I am proud of their desire to achieve, but my own desire to achieve has given my daughters a special classmate. I will be graduating from the Institute of American Indian Art in Santa Fe with them.

A few more passing suns will see
us here no more, and
our dust and bones will mingle
with these same prairies.

I see, as in a vision, the dying spark
of our council fires,
the ashes cold and white.

I see no longer the curling smoke
rising from our lodge poles.

I hear no longer the songs of the women
as they prepare the meal.

The antelope have gone; the buffalo
wallows are empty.
Only the wail of the coyote is heard.

The white man's medicine is stronger than ours;
his iron horse rushes over the buffalo trail.

He talks to us through his 'whispering spirit'
(the telephone).

We are like birds with a broken wing.
My heart is cold within me.
My eyes are growing dim—
I am old. . . .

—CHIEF PLENTY-COUPS,
CROW

A single twig breaks, but the
bundle of twigs is strong.
Someday I will embrace our brother
tribes and draw them
into a bundle and together, we
will win our country
back from the whites.

—TECUMSEH, SHAWNEE

THE WOODSHED WHEEL

Dave Risling, Hoopa, Karok, Yurok

In those days before cars came, there was just a wagon road to our house. We lived on what was then known as the Hoopa Reservation Extension in northern California. My dad worked in the woods and as a commercial fisherman, traveling 25 miles by river to the river mouth for supplies and work.

In my later growing-up years, we moved to be closer to the Hoopa Agency and School. My pop, David Risling Sr., was a born politician. Our house was a common meeting place for tribal discussion.

He always was an independent, get-it-done kind of guy. He ran away from the Chemawa Indian Boarding School near Salem, Oregon, in the third grade and learned to live on his own. Later, he picked up jobs in agriculture and construction and with the railroads. Someplace along the way, he learned to play the violin. I have many memories of my dad sawing away on his violin. He played for many of the fund-raising dances to help finance our fight with the federal government as it took our lands. Pop was always the best in everything he did.

I was an achiever in our high school. It was a little one, only 70 students, but I was student body president, captain of the football team and a champ boxer. Pop was the best in what he did, and I sure was going to try to be the same. This kept me away from the drinking. In our family, we also supplied all our own game, salmon and garden vegetables, and that kept me busy, too.

I was determined, the fall after finishing high school, to go on to college. There wasn't money for college, but I painted the school buildings during the summer at 25 cents an hour, and the savings began to grow. What really sealed the deal was when I was able to sell my two prize hogs for $66.

I was, therefore, pretty astonished when Pop invited me into the woodshed for a talk one August day, just prior to my leaving. Someone had surely told him a whopper of a story because I hadn't done anything wrong that I could think of.

The woodshed was to provide the backdrop for the greatest lesson I ever got. Pop looked me up and down and said, "You're leaving for college. Don't bother to come back if you forget who you are. And if you do come back, you better learn how to fight fire with fire, and understand the rights and laws we live by."

He drew a big circle on the dirt floor and put his stick right in the middle.

"Do you know what this is?" he asked.

"It's a circle with a dot in the center," I responded.

"That circle is the dominant society. The dot is us, and those are the odds you fight. In fact, we'd have to use our whole valley to symbolize the resources of the dominant society compared to the dot."

It was an awesome statistic. The sun had drifted through the window and the circle stood out, crudely drawn but making a point that I was never to forget.

"That world out there," he said, pointing to his circle, "is powerful, and making changes won't be easy." He paused, and I moved to go. I thought we were through.

His words stopped my movement. "Now make that circle a wheel. What do you have to do to help our people?"

I knew the answer. "I will be a lawyer."

He drew a line connecting the dot with the outside of the circle. "Do you think a wheel can turn with only one spoke?" I hadn't given the right answer.

"Well?" he probed.

I couldn't give him a good answer. That is when, in a dusty shed, on a remote California Indian reservation, I got the lesson that would guide me for the rest of my life.

"You need to have education away from here, and you need to understand everything you can about what is happening. Put in as many spokes as you can." At this point he stroked in half the wheel.

"But you also have to learn about your spirituality," and here he emphatically drew the first spoke on the other side of the wheel, "your culture and traditions," and the stick drew more spokes on the wheel.

"If you don't come home often and keep in touch, the

spokes won't be there. Some young people who leave here have problems coming back home. You need to keep the spokes on this side of your wheel full so it can roll right." His stick flashed out and drew in spokes. "Self-determination, control of your own education." With each item he listed, he drew in a spoke.

He emphasized the need for Native Americans to know their own history, do their own research, and even do their own printing, so the truth would be there. The stick continued to draw spokes.

"You can have information," he said, "but you have to know the channels to get things done." As I watched him draw in the dust, I was overwhelmed with both respect and love for this man who worked so hard to bring the best to his family and community.

I went to college, and it wasn't easy. I didn't have college prep classes or anything to prepare me for what I found there. I immediately went on academic probation and had to dig myself back out. There was only one other Native American in the school, from a reservation in Nevada, and he only stayed for a while.

Over time, life has put many spokes in my wheel. The wheel finally rolled out of the woodshed. It moved across California and even the nation. I am active in serving the cause of education for Native Americans.

But the wheel runs smoothly because its other side is full, too. I went back home often, as I still do, and did what I had always done with my dad: I helped organize the ceremonies. The White Deer Skin Dance comes in the fall and asks for world renewal. It is followed by the Jump Dance, ten days later, thanking the Creator for salmon, acorns, good life and the health of the people. For years I have worked to make sure it all comes off right: feeding all the people, checking ceremonial gear and contacting people who have disputes that must be dealt with before the ceremony can go on. There can be no bad thoughts, no disputes as people come to the ceremony.

As I have worked with Indian education and rights programs across the nation, I have always made sure that the wheels we create look like my dad's wheel on the woodshed floor.

LESSONS FROM THE TWO-HOLER

Darlene Brown Toyobo,
Concow/Yuki/Littlelake/Shoshone/Bannock

Most of the wisdom I have in this world came from long evenings at the old two-holer outhouse, where I went each evening with my grandmother. It was there that I was molded, developed and given the gift of positive thinking.

My grandparents raised me. My grandmother's name was Bernice Dorman Brown. She was a Yuki from the Round Valley Reservation in Covelo, California. People said we were poor, but I never felt that way. I had plenty to eat, was warm and dry, and had lots of love. We had no running water or indoor plumbing until I was 13. Gram hauled water every day, and on Sunday she heated water for my bath. She'd pull the curtains in the kitchen and pour the steaming water in a big round tub.

My hair was never cut as a child and I didn't wash my

Darlene Brown Toyobo

own hair. Gram did it. It was an act of great care and love to take my long black hair and shampoo it—even as I kicked and screamed as she worked out the snarls. My hair was both my own and my grandmother's great joy. Today I never touch my hair without thinking of Gram.

I used to brush my teeth every day at the horse trough. I guess that doesn't sound like the best way to brush your teeth, but every time I started, the horses would come over and stand there as I brushed. That's something I actually miss now when I brush my teeth at a sink.

One reason I never felt poor is that Gram never saw herself as poor. I never saw her complain. Her attitude in life was that you do what you have to do, live through the tough times, but most important, you grab the joy and happiness that life has to offer.

Those were the lessons of the two-holer. Each evening, either knowingly or unknowingly, she built my character. Everything she told me about living the most with what you have, she role-modeled for me. People seem to complain so much about the bad in life, but she always turned the bad around and made it good.

She'd gone to the Sherman Indian School in Riverside, California. The school had given her a lot of structure in life, as well as knowledge. From age four on, I was constantly impressed with the need to get as much education as I possibly could. It was a forceful message from the two-holer.

I tried to do what she said. Today I'm a successful publications manager for a printing house. I'm surrounded by editing and words all day. But to this day, the most powerful words are still those of the two-holer.

Darlene Brown Toyobo's grandparents,
Bernice Dorman and Colonel Brown, 1930s.

We respected our old people above
all others in the tribe.

To live to be so old, they must have
been brave and strong,
and good fighters, and we aspired to be like them.

We never allowed our old people to
want for anything. . . .

We looked upon our old people as
demigods of a kind,
and we loved them deeply.
They were all our fathers.

—Buffalo Child Long Lance, Sioux

JUST AN OLD HUMAN BEING

Cheewa James, Modoc

When the first whites came onto Modoc Oregon/California land in the mid 1800s, the Modoc tongue was difficult for them to manage. So they renamed the Modocs with whom they had contact.

Scarfaced Charley's name came from a large scar extending across his cheek. Black Jim was so named because even among Indians he was unusually dark. Boston Charley was very fair. Slat-us-locks became Steamboat Frank, named in recognition of his mother's resounding voice.

Ski-et-tete-ko, Left-handed Man, my father's grandfather, had a mother who was a very poor housekeeper, or so the story goes. So he was named Shacknasty Jim. That's still a hard one for me to live with if I choose to leave the dinner dishes overnight or don't catch all the cobwebs. In time, the Shacknasty part was dropped and the Jim elongated to James, now my last name.

My father always said the story about how we got our name wasn't true. The Shacknasty part, he said, was a corruption of a Modoc name of some sort. I guess we'll never know. My dad had a real thing about Indians being renamed by the whites, often in uncomplimentary ways, and urged Indian people to search their name origins.

My dad, who was a rancher, had different ideas of entertaining and caring for my brother, sister and me in the evenings or when we couldn't be outside. We lived on the Klamath Reservation in Oregon, and the inside of our house had the living room, dining room and kitchen connected in a circle. We three kids would line up "in the chute" and then come screeching through the living room where Daddy would rope us, gently, assuredly, bringing us down—just like was done with cattle at branding time. Then bellowing our lungs out, we'd circle back through the kitchen and dining room, into the chute again. What glorious rainy days we spent snorting and mooing like little calves.

My sister Doris was nine years older than the three of us, and I stood in great admiration of my very sophisticated, beautiful, "know-everything" teenager sister. Although she would never be caught running through the chute, she experienced my dad's rope, too.

She struck awe in the whole family when she appeared one evening, transformed into an elegantly-gowned princess, ready for her first formal dance. I knew she was nervous about the evening, and even more nervous when she saw that Daddy hadn't moved off the couch. My dad's hair had a slight wave to it, and when he washed it, he would wear a navy blue stocking cap to hold his hair down as it dried. There he sat, barefooted and wearing his blue cap.

He still sat on the couch when Doris' date, an equally nervous teenager, arrived. Daddy took one friendly look at the young man, corsage box in hand, and then showing the fine coordination that made him a great roper, grabbed his lasso, whipped it through the air and snagged the corsage box. I will always remember my sister's face. The elegant princess was not amused.

My father was born in 1900 in Oklahoma Indian Territory near the Quapaw Agency. He entered the Seneca Indian School at a very young age, and I have a picture of him in his military uniform with the BIA (Bureau of Indian Affairs) buttons running down the front.

Daddy was a gifted athlete from his earliest years. His sports took him into a world most American Indians didn't know. He went to college. From there, he played professional basketball through the 1920s and 30s. He was dubbed "Chief" James by his fellow players and played under that name, although he never was a chief. In fact, Modoc leaders were given the title "lagi," the term "chief" never existing.

As a contemporary of the great Indian football player Jim Thorpe, my dad was unique in his time as a professional basketball player. I remember as a young girl asking my dad how it felt to be out on the floor and have thousands of people chanting his name, "Chief James," "Chief James." How did it feel to be the only Indian out there and have all that accolade?

It was at that point that my father first showed me what human relationships were all about. He said, "I'm proud of my Indian blood, but we were a team, those guys and me. We were really a team. I never thought of myself as being all that different. In fact, I guess I thought of myself more as a human being. I'm just an old human being."

Many times, before he passed through the arch of life to the other side, my father would talk about being just an old human being. As an old human being, he had the ability to reach out and touch everybody. It didn't matter who they were, their economic level or ethnic background. He felt for everybody because they were human beings, too.

My father was just an old human being who passed on one of life's greatest gifts to his daughter: tolerance.

*Clyde James, 1907—Seneca Indian School,
Bureau of Indian Affairs school uniform.*

Clyde James, 1922, center,
Southwest Missouri State University Bears.

Old age was simply a delightful time,
when the old people sat playing in the sun
with the children until they fell asleep.

At last, they failed to wake up.

—JAYTIAMO, ACOMA

The old people came literally to love the soil, and they sat or reclined on the ground with a feeling of being close to a mothering power.

It was good for the skin to touch the earth, and the old people liked to remove their moccasins and walk with bare feet on the sacred earth.

Their tepees were built upon the earth and their altars were made of earth.

The birds that flew in the air came to rest upon the earth, and it was the final abiding place of all things that lived and grew.

The soul was soothing, strengthening, cleansing and healing.

That is why the old Indian still sits upon the earth instead of propping himself up and away from its life-giving forces.

For him, to sit or lie upon the ground is to be able to think more deeply and to feel more keenly.

He can see more clearly into the mysteries of life and come closer in kinship to other lives about him.

—CHIEF LUTHER STANDING BEAR,
TETON SIOUX

*What? Would you wish that there should be
no dried trees in the woods and no dead branches
on a tree that is growing old?*

—HURON

UMMIES AND OPPIES

Pam Pulsiser Gonzales, Wintun

I was raised by Ummie, which is short for *umachu*—grandmother in the Wintun language; and Oppie, short for *Opachu*—grandfather.

It seems a lot of us were raised by grandparents during a fragmented period of time that was particularly devastating to America Indian people. I'm certainly not a sociologist, but it seems that there was a tremendous reshuffling of lives and cultures. Many families were dysfunctional, and drinking was rampant.

Many older people took over child-raising responsibilities. Oppie died of tuberculosis when I was five. Though she was illiterate, Ummie was my light in life. She said she went to school one day and never went again. But as I started to read and write, it was my delight to try to teach her. She finally learned to write her name, but still used the old "X" when she went to town to get things.

My father was her only child, out of seven, to survive.

She wrapped me in cotton and took incredible care of me. She loved flowers and gardening, and one of the strongest memories I have of her was hearing her sing the old Wintun songs as she gardened. Why did so many of us lose the language? I guess we had other lives, were learning new things in school, and the Wintun language was not necessary for us to survive. It was only an interesting skill that our grandparents had. The last fluent speaker of Wintun died in 1992 at 95 years of age.

Those of us who came to our parents in that age of dysfunction often were delivered on doorsteps with scars. I never felt worthy of affection. Ummie gave me the incredibly great gift of self-esteem. She gave me unconditional love with no strings attached.

I know how my grandmother must have felt about me because I have a grandson now. He went to his first spring dance in the roundhouse and received his first blessing there. The spring dance is a time of hope for a fruitful summer. It is also a time of hope for human beings as they renew their understanding of life.

My hope is the same one Ummie had for me. Filled with unconditional love, generation after generation of Ummies and Oppies bless their offspring as they lift their shoulders and walk the path of life.

There was a time when our people
covered the land as the
waves of a wind-ruffled sea cover
its shell-paved floor.
But that time long since passed. . . .
Our people are ebbing away like a rapidly
receding tide that will never return. . . .

Tribe follows tribe, and nation follows nation,
like the waves of the sea. It is the order
of nature, and regret is useless.

Your time of decay may be distant, but it will
certainly come, for even the White Man, whose
God walked and talked with him as friend with
friend, cannot be exempt from the common destiny.

We may be brothers after all. We will see. . . .

Even the rocks, which seem to be dumb and
dead as they swelter in the sun along the silent
shore, thrill with memories of stirring events
connected with the lives of my people, and the
very dust upon which you now stand responds
more lovingly to their footsteps than to

*yours because it is rich with the dust of our
ancestors, and our bare feet are conscious
of the sympathetic touch. . . .*

*And when the last Red Man shall have
perished and the memory of my tribe shall have
become a myth among the White Man, these
shores will swarm with the invisible dead
of my tribe, and when your children's children
think themselves alone in the fields, the store,
the shop, upon the highway or in the silence of the
pathless woods, they will not be alone. . . .*

*At night when the streets of your villages and cities
are silent and you think them deserted, they
will throng with the returning hosts that once
filled them and still love this beautiful land.*

*The White Man will never be alone.
Let him be just and deal kindly with my people,
for the dead are not powerless.*

*Death, I say? There is no death.
Only a change of worlds.*

—Duwamish thought, attributed
by some to Chief Seattle

When your time comes to die,
be not like those whose hearts are filled with
the fear of death; when their time comes, they
weep and pray for a little more time to
live their lives over again in
a different way.

Sing your death song, and die like
a hero going home.

—TECUMSEH, SHAWNEE

LAKOTA WAYS

Wynn Dubray, Rosebud Sioux

I have raised my children with the help of my mother. My mother died several years ago, but she comes back regularly in my dreams with advice and help. She is very literal and quite clear in what she says. She is there. It is so real that when I wake, I am filled with disappointment that she is gone. A couple of times, when she felt I was in danger with certain people, she named them and asked me to move away from them. And she was absolutely right.

My mother and I shared a common birth date. We were very close. I was her eighth child. I was young when she died, and I feel she has taken this way to offer her guidance. She has continued to help me with my grandchildren.

Intuition and metaphysics are a natural part of my culture. My father had strong psychic abilities. After dinner, in good weather, our family would often gather in a circle outside. For 43 years my parents lived together in the same house, on the Rosebud Sioux land in South Dakota.

My father, Peter DuBray, made predictions about the weather, the kind of crops that would prosper in a given year, and the people who would come to visit us. It came about as he said. I didn't give it a thought, because when that is all you know, it is the life you accept. My father's actions were very normal. As I grew older, I began to realize that there were things Indian people shared with each other and did not share with whites in the area. I learned to cross back and forth continually between the two worlds.

I was blessed with visionary parents who understood that their ten children would face tremendous changes. They prepared us to survive. Between them, they created a strong, stable family.

My mother, Lillian, was orphaned at nine. Around the turn of the century, she went away to school at the St. Mary's Indian School on the extended Rosebud Reservation, then to Carlisle Indian Boarding School in Pennsylvania. She stayed at Carlisle until she was 22, working as an indentured servant. When she returned, she married my father and moved to our home, located in the outlying areas of South Dakota Indian land between Winner and Presho.

My mother never worked outside the home, but she had the sophistication to know her parenting would have to be unique if it was to guide us through the new and changing world ahead. She was one of the healthiest people—mentally, spiritually and emotionally—I have ever known. She was a dedicated mother and homemaker. She and my father were both fluent in their native language, and she accepted her role, as a woman's responsibility, to pass on our traditional teachings. She never drank or smoked, never cut her hair or wore make-up. She beaded moccasins and jewelry. She was happy, giving and patient and, by just observing her, I learned how to relate to people and to move away from fear. She taught me to take risks.

One of the great lessons she gave to her children was the respect for all life: not just people, but also plants, birds, animals, everything around us. We lived on a big ranch and there was a large spring on our property surrounded by trees. We often walked there, and she would have us listen to birds' singing as we went. She told us we should walk often among birds and animals and experience the connections among us all.

I didn't realize until I left the reservation how different our culture was from the one I was about to enter. The whole idea of healing, practiced in our ceremonies, was so clear. My mother and father, as their parents before them, had a strong sense of enlightenment and destiny.

My father planned his own funeral. Three days before his death, he expressed a sense of joy that he would be leaving. My mother comforted the whole family and helped ease us through this time.

They both believed that in the afterlife, the soul continues to live. The spirit stays earthbound for one year. During that year, a spirit-keeper is designated by the family to prepare for the "give away," a ceremony at the end of the year. At that time, items hand-made by the family are given away to others, and the departed spirit is released to go beyond to the other world.

I have a doctorate in psychology, teach university graduate students and have a private practice. The love my parents gave me and the values of my people are always there for me. The Lakota philosophy and values and the love of my family have guided me throughout my life. I am very proud to be a Lakota.

At the edge of the cornfield a bird
will sing with them
in the oneness of their happiness.

So they will sing together in tune with the
universal power, in harmony with the
one Creator of all things.

And the bird song, and the people's song, and
the song of life will become one.

—SONG OF THE LONG HAIR KACHINAS, HOPI

*May serenity circle on silent wings and
catch the whisper of the wind.*

—CHEEWA JAMES, MODOC

Share the Magic of Chicken Soup